THE GREAT N &
GREAT E
JOINT R

(March to Doncaster)

By
C. T. GOODE

1989
ISBN 1 870313 06 2
72 Woodland Drive, Anlaby, Hull. HU10 7HX.

Contents

Foreword

Strange, perhaps, but the subject of this little book seems to have escaped the attentions of railway historians in the past, probably because it was a hybrid mix of two great concerns and fell between the two. Like several other latecomers on the railway scene, such as the Great Central extension to London and the Hull & Barnsley, it has fallen foul of Rationalisation and largely lost its separate identity. I am happy to have made acquaintance with the GN & GE Joint,or 'Swedey' as it was known at Doncaster where I spent my early days being dazzled by the products of Gorton, impressed (and deafened) by those of my native heath and singularly unaware of this particular line, apart from a rather timid incursion from time to time by one of Holden's goods engines into Hexthorpe Top yard, usually during an odd afternoon during the last war.

I hope readers will feel moved, as I was, to look up Stow Park, Potterhanworth or Spalding before it is too late. Warmest acknowledgements to the Great Eastern Railway Society, and the Lincolnshire Library service for assistance freely given.

C. Tony Goode.

Anlaby, Hull. 1989.

Designed & Printed by
Swannack Brown & Co. Ltd.,
13a Anlaby Road, Hull.

The GN &GE Joint Railway

Chapter 1

This is another story of uneasy bedfellows; the Great Northern Railway who were enterprising and empire-building, with legitimate ideas of gaining traffic from the North towards the Capital and of expanding in every possible direction, and the Great Eastern Railway, a more parochial concern rooted in East Anglia, not in any way as prosperous as the former and ultimately fired with the idea of reaching the coalfields of South Yorkshire through Lincolnshire, thereby gaining an outlet to the North, a move which would thereby place the two companies in a state of rivalry. The GER was at first chary of entering into any form of joint working with the GNR, and as early as September 1864 had entered into an agreement with the Lancashire & Yorkshire Railway, a system which had no link with London, to draw up plans for a railway of 113 miles to run from Askern at the Doncaster end of the branch from Knottingley, then by way of Peterborough and Lincoln to Long Stanton in Cambridgeshire. A 13 mile branch from Haxey to Goole was to be thrown in, foreshadowing the later Axholme Joint Railway which materialised containing an L & Y element. The capital sum needed, of £1½ million, was to be raised equally by each company and running powers were equally divided, with the L & Y enjoying entry to Liverpool Street. There was, as expected, vigorous opposition from the GNR, chiefly over the possibility that coal would be transported at much cheaper rates than it could itself offer. The rate for construction, at £12,000 per mile was also queried, and the Bill succumbed after a second Reading on 14th. March 1865.

The GER thus showed the GNR its mettle. In 1863 it promoted a Bill to extend the March to Spalding line, a move which was acceptable if it allowed the GNR running powers to Doncaster. The GNR proposed a Bill extending the line from Spalding to March, equally acceptable to the other party if running were to be allowed to the GER, all in a sort of tit-for-tat arrangement.

On a grander scale the GNR proposed to extend its Peterborough-Boston-Lincoln-Gainsborough loop to Doncaster, cutting out the run to Retford over the Manchester, Sheffield & Lincolnshire Company's line from Sykes Jc., north of Lincoln. Thus, a part of what was to be the Joint Line, that from Gainsborough to Doncaster was to come into being, with a through route also available to Doncaster from March via Boston. The GNR offered running powers to the GER for mineral traffic only between Spalding and Doncaster, a move which was not sufficiently attractive as the GER had all along wished for direct links with the South Yorkshire coalfield. Thus a counter proposal arose that they should build, with the GNR, a loop running between Spalding and Gainsborough, and that the lines between March and Spalding and Gainsborough and Doncaster should be jointly owned. The GNR gave its approval and put in hand the March to Spalding section which was opened on 1st. April 1867 and the Doncaster to Gainsborough line, opened on 15th. July 1867. For access to Gainsborough the GNR managed to use the MS & L crossing of the Trent just outside the town, paying the appropriate tolls.

On the surface, then, all seemed to be well between the two companies, the GNR and GER, and they were set to build a new direct line from Spalding to Lincoln. However, the GER were suffering from a certain amount of financial embarrassment, to such an extent that the shareholders ousted the directoral body and elected others who blocked the scheme and brought matters almost back to square one. There were proposals to fuse the two companies together, but these foundered on terms of agreement.

One year fixed for amalgamation was 1883, subject to a thorough inspection of the GER permanent way, signalling and the like. Things were obviously on the ramshackle side as no agreement could be reached on what must be done to bring things up to standard. The sum of £1½ million was mentioned and the idea of union was forgotten once the GER demanded a 6% dividend to be guaranteed for ten years.

Class B1 No. 61250 leaves Spalding on the joint line with a Down express. *P. H. Wells*

In 1872 overtures were again made by the GER for running powers and joint ownership, with an idea put forward by the GNR for joint working on all lines between Shepreth Jc. (near Cambridge) and Doncaster, and the building of a separate new line between Shepreth and March and Spalding and Lincoln. The GNR also required copious running powers as part of the package, namely over lines between Huntingdon and Cambridge and Newmarket, and from Ely to Yarmouth and Norwich.

Needless to say, the GER rejected these.

The ball was now in the GER's court and in 1878 it revised the earlier scheme to link up with the L & YR by building its own line through Sleaford and Lincoln to Askern, from whence it would convey cheap coal. This incensed the GNR once more, causing them to counter with their own proposal for a direct line from Spalding to Lincoln via Sleaford, this time withdrawing demands for running powers to Norwich and Yarmouth but suggesting that the Joint line start at Huntingdon. It was now the turn of the GER to jib furiously, taking the matter into parliamentary debate and losing the contest.

Things reached a kind of plateau when the GNR Spalding-Lincoln scheme was approved in exchange for the GER being allowed to have running powers as far as Doncaster, and a settlement was finally attained in 1879 when the Joint Line Bill was drawn up for a system of lines, running from Huntingdon to Black Carr Jc. near Doncaster, via St. Ives, March, Spalding, Sleaford, Lincoln and Gainsborough, the concern to be managed by a joint committee of five directors of each company. Of the two, the GER probably benefitted more and made every effort to win traffic, while the GNR lost revenue from exchange traffic formerly handled at March, Peterborough and Huntingdon, which now went by the Joint line, up to £50,000 in the first months of operation. However, to the GNR directors the new route was a long-term investment.

Officially, then, the Joint Committee existed as from 3rd. July 1879, administering a line of hybrid antecedents as follows:

	Huntingdon to St. Ives. East Anglian Railway of 1847
	Needingworth Jc. to March, Eastern Counties Railway of 1848
	March to Spalding, Great Northern Railway of 1867
plus a new	Spalding to Ruskington line of 1878 (opened 6th. March 1882)
and a new	Ruskington to Lincoln line of 1878 (opened 1st. August 1882)
and lastly	Lincoln to Black Carr Jc. Great Northern Railway of 1867

Three directors from each company met at the first committee meeting on 11th. August 1879, with Mr. C. H. Parkes of the GER as Chairman. The first Manager of the line was J. Crabtree of the Colne Valley line who was appointed at £600 per annum.

Chapter 2

As the reader will have noted, Ruskington formed the boundary between the two sections of line constructed from Lincoln to Spalding, with R. Johnson the Engineer of the northern section and A. Langley responsible for the section south of Ruskington. The No. 1 contract from Spalding to Ruskington, of 20 miles 40 chains went to Kirk & Parry for £147,760 on 26th. February 1880, while No. 2 contract from Ruskington to Lincoln was awarded to Baker & Firbank for £230,233 on 19th. March 1880.

Works on the No. 1 contract were light, and the only major task was the lowering of the GNR Sleaford to Boston line where the new Joint line was to cross it. Both Sleaford and Spalding stations were rebuilt and resignalled, and contractor's temporary lines laid in. Resignalling went to McKenzie & Holland on the March to Spalding line, while Saxby & Farmer signalled north of Ruskington and Stevens & Son south of that point. Once the GNR lines involved had been transferred to the new Joint committee on 6th. March 1882, then the Spalding-Ruskington section of line was opened. The contract for eleven stations and appurtenances took up £62,842 and went to Pattinson, subject to economies with platform awnings and the like.

Sleaford station was avoided to the east by the new line, though to enable trains to call there spurs were put in from new cabins at Sleaford South Jc. to East Jc. of 39 chains and from West Jc. to North Jc. of 2 miles 9 chains. Latterly the section of main Joint line which by-passed Sleaford has been

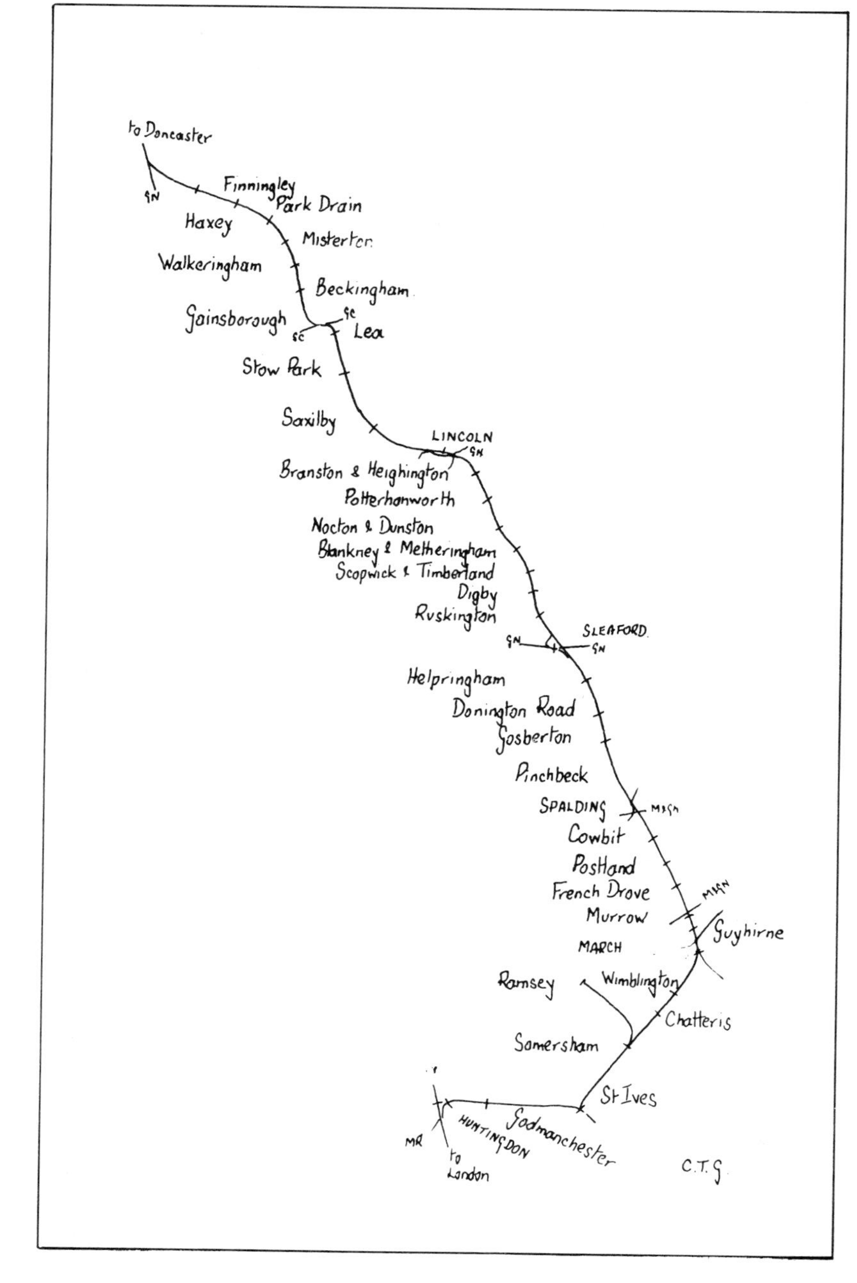
to Doncaster
GN
Finningley
Park Drain
Haxey
Misterton
Walkeringham
Beckingham
Gainsborough
GC
GC
Lea
Stow Park
Saxilby
LINCOLN
GN
Branston & Heighington
Potterhanworth
Nocton & Dunston
Blankney & Metheringham
Scopwick & Timberland
Digby
Ruskington
GN
SLEAFORD
GN
Helpringham
Donington Road
Gosberton
Pinchbeck
SPALDING
M&GN
Cowbit
Postland
French Drove
M&GN
Murrow
Guyhirne
MARCH
Ramsey
Wimblington
Chatteris
Somersham
St Ives
Godmanchester
HUNTINGDON
MR
to London
C.T.G.

Official postcard of Potterhanworth. Note the split name and full station awnings. *A. Foster*

closed, necessitating all traffic passing round the spurs and through the station. The station was first opened on the Boston, Sleaford & Midland Countries Railway from Grantham on 16th. June 1857, the line reaching Boston on 13th. April 1859. The place became a junction on 2nd. January 1872 when the line to Bourne was opened. An additional feature of interest was the branch to Cranwell of January 1916, where the Admiralty had founded a naval air station. It was arranged that they would pay for the five mile branch from a junction just west of Sleaford West Jc., a light railway under GNR aegis. This was opened in 1917, just a year before the Royal Flying Corps became the RAF.

On the section of line from Spalding to Ruskington there was one viaduct of four arches, 21 overbridges and the overbridge for the GNR Boston line at Sleaford with a span of 68 feet. The ruling gradient was 1 in 200. There were many level crossings, and the important ones between Spalding and Sleaford are given here, as some of the names are intriguing and sonorous:

Mill Green, Blue Gowts, Cherry Holt, Flax Mill, Beaty Fen, No. 94 Water Drove, Cheal Road, Brewery Lane, Quadring, Church Lane, Golden High Hedges, Malting Lane and Blotoft Siding.

Spalding station had of course a worthy ancestry, being on the original 1848 Peterborough, Boston and Lincoln route until the Towns line appeared in 1852. The line to March opened on 1st. April 1867. On 15th. November 1858 Norwich & Spalding Railway opened a line from Spalding to Holbeach, extended to Sutton Bridge on 1st. July 1862. Thereafter the Bourne line was opened on 1st. August 1866. With the opening of the Saxby to Bourne line on

5th. June 1893 (to passengers from 1st. May 1894) the Midland Railway began to make its presence felt in the area, and the Midland & Great Northern Joint line began to move passengers between the Midlands, Kings Lynn and the Norfolk coast. As at Sleaford, spurs were put in at Spalding to enable trains to call there, though through traffic could pass directly east-west unhindered south of the town. In its heyday the station was big and busy, with King's Cross-Grimsby, M & GN and Joint line services all cheek by jowl.

Stations for Railway No. 1 were at Pinchbeck, Gosberton, Donington Road, Helpringham and, north of Sleaford, Ruskington.

Chapter 3

Railway No. 2 from Lincoln (Sincil Jc.) was of 16 miles 4 chains and ran to an avoiding line passing Lincoln on the south west side from Greetwell West Jc. for a little over three miles to Pyewipe Jc. On this west side a short spur ran from Boultham Jc. round to West Holmes Jc. which enabled GN goods traffic to reach the yards without fouling the station area and its level crossings at each end. The No. 2 contract had a good share of embarkments and cuttings, 31 bridges and one three span viaduct, but only three level crossings. By its nature the Avoiding line had several underbridges and two longish viaducts. Stations north from Ruskington were Digby, Scopwick & Timberland, Blankney & Metheringham, Nocton & Dunston and Heighington for Branston which was changed to Branston & Heighington from May 1884.

Class B17 No. 61621 "Hatfield House" passes Cowbit on the express.
Douglas Thompson

On 6th. June 1883 a short spur of one mile in length chiefly on viaduct was opened by the GNR from Washingborough Jc. to Greetwell East Jc., constructed by Baker & Firbank. This enabled all GNR goods workings to avoid passing through Lincoln station. The line was closed from 25th. May 1884 to 20th. July 1885 to rectify damage caused by subsidence.

Goods working used the Joint line first of all from 1st. July 1882 with the GNR providing a working to Lincoln. Then, on 1st. August 1882 the Avoiding line opened for goods at the same time as the main line saw its first passenger trains, when the GNR inaugurated a through service to Doncaster. At this time the northern stretch of line from Pyewipe Jc. to Black Carr Jc. passed into Joint ownership. From 20th. March 1883 the Avoiding line at Lincoln could be used by passenger trains when required under absolute block regulations. Administration was by the GNR north of the crossing with the Sleaford to Boston line, with the GER handling the southern portion. The GNR worked the booking offices at Sleaford and Spalding; the GER at St. Ives and March.

Chapter 4

March was, and still is in several respects, one of the king pins in the railway system in East Anglia. The place was, originally, a fenland village with life centred round the river here, and considered as a stopping place by the Eastern Counties Railway on its new line from Ely to Peterborough, opened on 14th. January 1847, to connect with the London & North Western branch

LNER Class D9 4-4-0 No. 5112 at March shed. *Colling Turner*

Blankney and Metheringham station. *Douglas Thompson*

from Blisworth to Peterborough, thus bringing an exchange of traffic between East Anglia and the Midlands. As often happens in such cases, the course of the line was set to pass through cheaper land away from habitation; in the case of March to the north of the village, with the result that the town developed as a sprawl to the station from the old village centre. Originally a Roman settlement, the population of the town rose to 7,565 by 1901, and to 14,285 by 1971 with a penchant for general and agricultural engineering locally. A new civic building was provided in 1900 to keep counsel with the church of Saint Wendreda, rather obscure but probably the patron saint of marshalling yards.

Successively, the line to Wisbech was opened in1847 and to St. Ives one year later, laying down the beginnings of an important junction with exchange sidings. The line to Spalding, our Joint line, generated much local farm traffic, if not many passengers, though, as will be seen later, it carried heavy northern goods workings from the yards at March which were four in number, vast and uneconomic up to 1925. The LNER implemented a scheme costing £285,000 to provide a new gravity worked Up yard with the first rail retarders to be used in Britain. This was opened in 1929, cutting down the handling time of wagons and providing new freight services for London, East Anglia and the Midlands. Wartime saw, of course, a surge in use with one day in August 1942 seeing 59 trains passing over the Up hump. Use of the yards increased after the end of hostilities, with a possible capacity of both yards of 7,000 wagons per day and the installation of radio telephones for communication. By 1977, however, the former 68 acre site had been reduced, as had the appearance of many wagons, now down to 1,700 or so. The original sidings, stabling and tranship shed had been open from September 1869, known first as March Joint, while the name Whitemoor came into being from

1st. July 1882. At Whitemoor in 1883 were a station master's house and twelve cottages.

March station was itself at one time busy, with up to 5,000 sacks of parcels and mail being handled each day. This traffic went ultimately to a new depot at Peterborough. Mention should be made of the considerable volume of Campbell's soup traffic at March from King's Lynn.

In November 1884 the GER put in a western spur at March for through running between Peterborough and northern destinations.

The line from March to Spalding, the result of rivalry between the GNR and GER, went to the GNR by an Act of 21st. July 1863 with running powers awarded to the latter. It opened for goods traffic on 11th. April 1867 and to passengers in September of that year, running officially from Grassmoor Jc. (Whitemoor) as from 1897 to enable a yard at that point to be transferred from GNR to GER ownership. The course of the line to Spalding was uninteresting, with stations at Guyhirn (sometimes Guyhirne), Murrow, French Drove, Postland and Cowbit. Refuge sidings were put in at Murrow and French Drove in 1883. Goods depots were opened at Twenty Foot River, north of Grassmoor, and at Guyhirn on 1st. December 1869.

Ex GCR 4-6-0 LNER No. 6099 on shed. *W. L. Good*

Chapter 5

Lincoln was already established as a railway centre long before the Joint line had come into being, with the Midland Railway arriving in an unlikely way from Nottingham and Newark on 3rd. August 1846. The visit was followed by

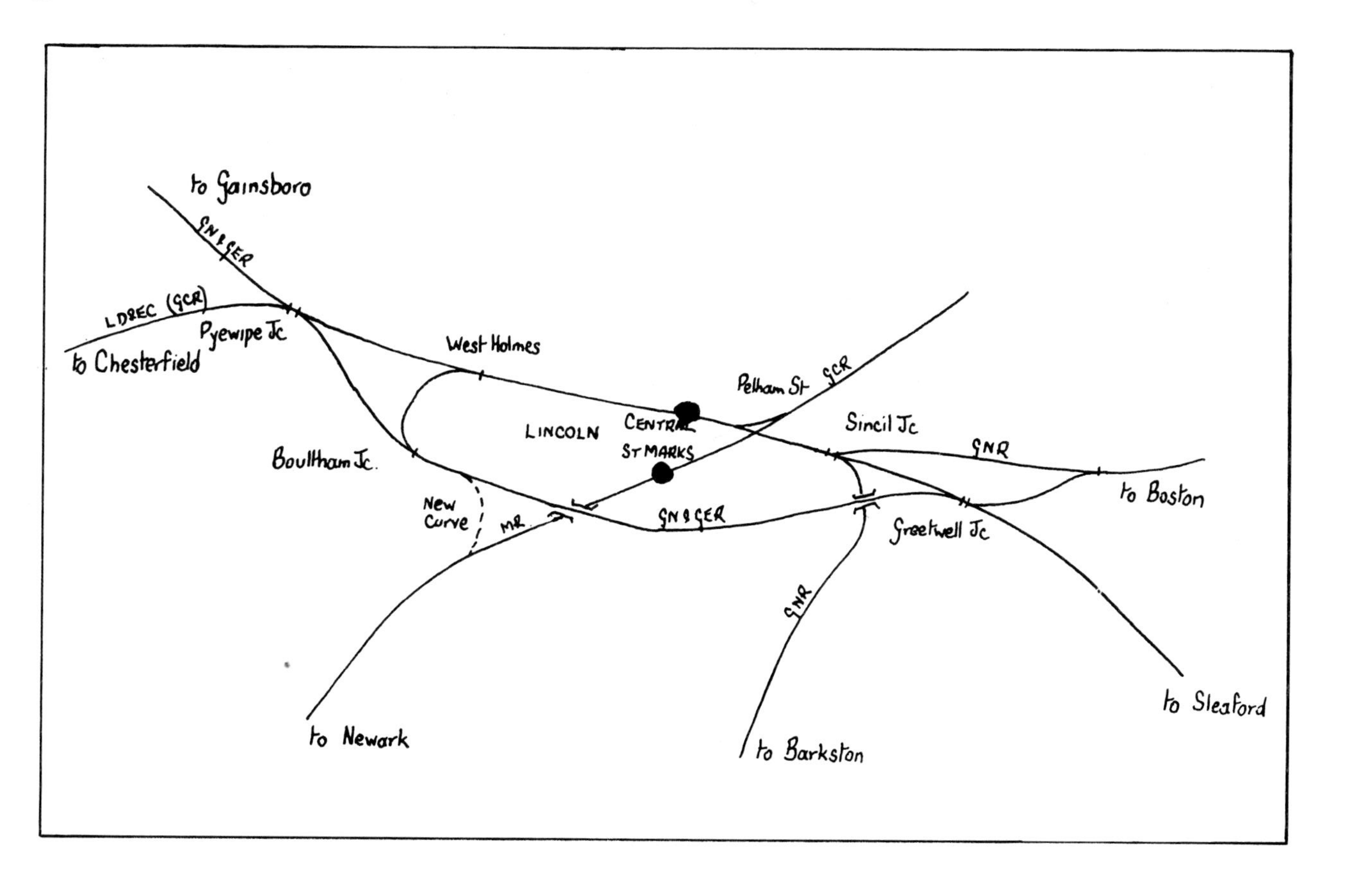
to Gainsboro
GN&GER
LD&EC (GCR)
Pyewipe Jc
to Chesterfield
West Holmes
Pelham St
GCR
CENTRAL
LINCOLN
ST MARKS
Sincil Jc
GNR
Boultham Jc.
to Boston
New Curve
MR
GN&GER
Greetwell Jc
GNR
to Newark
to Barkston
to Sleaford

the GNR Loop line from Boston on 17th. October 1848, extending north to Gainsborough on 9th. April 1849. The third arrival was by the MS & L on its line from Grimsby and Market Rasen, on 18th. December 1848, which executed a flat crossing of the GNR just outside their station and made an end-on connection with the MR just outside theirs. Shortly after the three had settled down more or less amicably in the city, the GNR and MS & L were enabled, by a short spur, to run between their two systems, thus complicating the area of the flat crossing, which also carried a public roadway, even further. From 9th. April 1849 the line out to Gainsborough gave access to Retford over the MS & L, while a cut-off line to Retford via Sykes Jc. near Saxilby, and Clarborough Jc. was opened on 7th. August 1850.

Other developments to be mentioned were the opening of lines to the Coast via Bardney on 1st. December 1876, and the somewhat late arrival of the Lancashire, Derbyshire & East Coast Railway from Chesterfield to Pyewipe Jc. on 8th. March 1897. Graced by all this flattering attention, Lincoln city prospered, with heavy industry flourishing alongside its markets and with household names such as Clayton Dewandre, Shuttleworth, Robey and Ruston & Hornsby featuring prominently in its life.

Irritated by early GER proposals for a joint line and for extensions of its own, the GNR also opened a line to Honington on 15th. April 1867 as part of a possible route from East Anglia to the north. Trains on this line also reached the GNR station by way of the flat crossing. However, as the reader will know, the Joint line gained its Act of 1879, with GER passenger trains being allowed to run via the GNR station but not goods trains, a move made largely because of approaches by the city council who wished to cut down road hold-ups at the two main level crossings at each end of the station. This was the raison d'être of the Avoiding line running to the south and west of the city, a high level affair giving goods trains a clear run free of the level crossings, and to which GNR goods workings came from 7th. June 1883 when the Washingborough spur was opened. At the west end, where the Avoiding line came down, a small yard was set up at Pyewipe, chiefly for the exchange of GER traffic, but also useful for later LD & ECR freight forwarding.

An Act of 26th. June 1846 brought into being the section of railway known as the Lincolnshire Loop, running initially alongside the Fossdyke Navigation towards Gainsborough and as far as the spot later called Sykes Jc. where the MS & L cut-off line to Retford went off to the west side. This line was straight, level and of double track, having a station on it opened on 1st. January 1865 called Skellingthorpe to serve a manure works. This soon closed in 1868, however, the siding being retained and renamed Kesteven in 1897. Beyond Sykes Jc. things changed, for the line to Gainsborough had noticeable gradients and appears to have been single along seven miles or so, probably to save expense. It was doubled after having been open for about ten years. Looking ahead to the projection of the route through Gainsborough to Doncaster, it was decided to revamp the existing line and, in particular, to iron out the gradients to some extent, lowering the formation by twenty feet or so at Lea station, south of Gainsborough, which sank the platforms into a cutting, an unusual feature for the Joint line and which left the station building high up at road level. GNR trains had been the first to reach Gainsborough from Lincoln, with the MS & L arriving next from Grimsby on 2nd. April 1850 and then on to Sheffield in July of that year. GNR trains had to run to and from the MS & L station, until a curve was put in from south to west to bring trains round to cross the Trent rail bridge, and a fine new station was provided on this curve at a rather awkward location for operating purposes as a branch line led straight on from the platform ends and down beneath the MS & L to a wharf on the Trent, opened 1st. March 1871, while alongside this branch quite congested industrial development took place. In order to shave off the peaks on this stretch of line, closure took place from 1st. December 1864 to 1st. July 1867 at which time the Gainsborough to Doncaster line also opened. From Sykes Jc. the line fell at 1 in 400 for three miles to Stow Park, followed by three miles at 1 in 200 to Lea, with a succeeding 1 in 400 descent into Gainsborough. Improvements were made to the amenities at Gainsborough station in 1883, with resignalling in 1895 and lengthening of the platforms at the turn of the century. Today the GNR station retains atmosphere, while the once impressive MS & L premises are now two bus shelters.

Chapter 6

The Gainsborough to Doncaster section of the 'loop' line was authorised on 25th. July 1864, and this also covered the alterations hitherto mentioned in preparation for the extension, as well as for a separate crossing of the Trent. The latter was, however, considered as being an unnecessary expense and the existing bridge was used by agreement with the owning company. The through route opened for passenger services on 15th. July 1867 along a line which was level and unspectacular, running generally north west to Haxey, where it then took a more westerly direction to Black Carr Jc. on the GNR parent line at Doncaster, with a final rise to Finningley en route.

Renumbered LNER Class B8 4-6-0 No. 1355 transfers a heavy goods train south of York. *C. Ord*

Stow Park station and signal box. *C. T. Goode*

Near Misterton, a surprisingly large village for the area, the engineering company of Morris at Stockwith on the Trent nearby asked the GNR to build a tramway to serve their works, this in October 1877. The company agreed at a cost of £933, plus £300 for a siding and wharf. The whole was opened in 1881 and was served from Misterton station site by a fall to exchange sidings on the east side.

Great things were obviously expected at Haxey, where the rather ambitious Isle of Axholme Light Railway ended up after a long and lonely single line excursion down from Goole to the north. The line was vested jointly in the L & Y and North Eastern companies and ran though no place of great merit except, perhaps, for Crowle, from which point it opened as from 3rd. November 1904 to its own station at Haxey Jc. cheek by jowl with Haxey Jc. on the Joint line and connected by a back shunt. Much later still an even more nebulous line ran from Bawtry on the GNR main line to Haxey across nowhere in particular as part of a plan to link the new collieries around Harworth and Tickhill in South Yorkshire with the Joint line. Construction was much delayed from conception in 1902, and eventually a goods train ran as from 26th. August 1912. Possibly both the new lines in question were laid in advance of prospecting for coal which was sought for a time in the vicinity of Park Drain, where there was originally a goods siding before the isolated station was opened on 2nd. March 1896.

The railway history of Doncaster and its surroundings makes a small book in its own right, and this was already a town of some importance as a trading and staging post on the old Roman road before railways were thought of. The development of the Barnsley coalfield to the west stimulated railway growth, helped by a mass of cheap land available nearby on the flat and marshy Carrs which was convenient for the building of marshalling yards. The first line to reach the area was a part of the L & YR from Knottingley to Askern, a mining village to the north of Doncaster, opened on 6th. June 1848 and making an end-on junction with a line built by the GNR from Askern to Doncaster and opened on 5th. August 1848. The line of route was projected southwards to Retford and opened on 4th. September 1849, thus giving a through run by means of the route already mentioned, that is via Retford, the MS & L, Lincoln, Peterborough and the Eastern Countries Railway. The South Yorkshire Railway began to bring coal from the Barnsley area after opening of its line from the Midland Railway at Swinton on 10th. November 1849. By the end of 1855 the long stretch of the GNR 'towns' line from Peterborough to Retford was open for business, and thus the main through corridor to London and north to York via Knottingley and Burton Salmon was available.

As mentioned, the Joint line joined the GNR proper at Black Carr Jc., and the patchwork of yards for the remaining two or three miles into Doncaster station had little that was essentially 'joint line' about them, except for a small GER shed south of the main GNR premises on the Up side of the line.

Chapter 7

There was only one new section of Joint line constructed, namely that between Spalding and Lincoln, the rest being simply railways which existed and which were transferred to the Committee as they stood. The trickiest portions of this survey have been saved until later; these were at the south end of the system and involved the short section from Huntingdon to St. Ives and from Needingworth Jc. north of that town to March.

First line in the field was the Ely & Huntingdon Railway, brought into being by an Act of 30th. June 1845. This should be taken along with the floating of the line proposed by the Eastern Counties Railway from Cambridge through St. Ives to March and Wisbech, which was sanctioned in 1845 along with running powers over the new line to Huntingdon from St. Ives when completed. The E & H set to work on the construction of this section; in the event they never completed their line as far as Ely. The first terminus of the E & H line was on the east bank of the Great Ouse (later Godmanchester), the run being single with facilities for double track. The line was opened on 17th. August 1847 concurrent with the Cambridge to St. Ives line, and at about this time the E & H became part of the East Anglian Railway, a move which did little for their finances, with the result that the big and rather wolfish GNR nearly agreed to take over the working of the EAR. This involved extending the line west from the terminus to the GNR premises across the Great Ouse. The new double track was opened on 29th. October 1851.

The Midland arrived on the scene in February 1866 when the Kettering, Thrapston & Huntingdon Railway, worked by them, reached Huntingdon to join the EAR (now GER) by way of the two stations, operating goods and passenger services between Kettering and Cambridge from March 1866. There was also a somewhat vague connection between the MR and the GNR line at Huntingdon.

Envisaged in the Joint line Act of 1879 was the rebuilding of the link between the two stations at Huntingdon and a doubling of the line to St. Ives. The latter was only achieved in the Huntingdon area, as far as the original terminus which was renamed Godmanchester in 1882. The west station at Huntingdon became the Joint station on 1st. July 1883, and the doubling came into use from 7th. August 1884. As far as the complete Joint line was concerned, this southern section had little effect and was hardly more than a minor cross country route.

The section from St. Ives to March was opened to goods on 1st. February 1848 and to passengers a month later, with an immediate flow of traffic in grain from the St. Ives market northwards to Wisbech over the line from March which had opened a year earlier. At an intermediate station, Chatteris, a dock was located on the 40 Foot Drain to provide a quicker supply of goods between fenland mills and farms, such as coal, fertiliser and grain. Perhaps rather surprising was the establishment of an ironworks at Chatteris in 1890. Other intermediate stations were Somersham and Wimblington, while there was a junction south of Somersham with the GER line from Ely and, north of the station, a junction with the branch to Ramsey High Street (later East), opened in September 1889 and taken over completely by the Joint line from 1897. The line in question was suitably upgraded on being taken over by the Joint concern from 1881, with some of the wooden and cast iron bridges rebuilt in wrought iron in anticipation of the heavy traffic which would ensue.

Chapter 8

At Huntingdon, some 59 miles north of King's Cross on the main line, a sizeable layout had developed around the station which lay to the west of the town and which had opened for traffic on 7th. August 1850, the goods facilities coming into use in the following December. By the 1920s the station had acquired a down island platform, though for many years after, the station formed a bottleneck for Up trains until they reached widening at the south end. There were two signal boxes, and at the South junction the line from St. Ives came in southwards, with the Joint line station of Huntingdon which became Huntingdon East in 1923 when the GNR line version became North. The station was opened on 1st. May 1883, was on a curve at the junction and had an island platform on the south side outer face served MR trains coming up by way of the single line which passed beneath the GNR main line from the Kettering direction, arriving behind the South Jc. signal box. The platforms had ample awnings and gas lighting in the best GNR style. Goods facilities, however, were few, with a turntable on the north side of the layout.

Hard by the junction with the main line was the river, and this had to be crossed again before Godmanchester station (¾ mile) was reached, an affair with staggered platforms and signal box on the north side controlling a small goods yard, cornmill and dock. The goods shed here was on the south side. The layout was somewhat cramped by the presence of the Ouse river which creates a peninsular at this point, the railway having to cross yet again at the eastern side. The main road, Ermine Street, also passed north-south to the

'FLY' TO FINNINGLEY!

WITH BRITISH RAIL

Ease the strain and travel by train to Britain's largest single-day Airshow and **reduce** the normal Adult admission charge from £4 to **£3!** OAP's and Children (8- 16) £1.
Children under 8 admitted Free!

British Rail and the RAF have combined to bring you this special discount which is available when you purchase your all inclusive rail and airshow ticket at your local BR station. Travel in comfort **direct** to the show arriving at our custom built platform actually within the airfield boundary.

Enquire at your local BR station for further details.

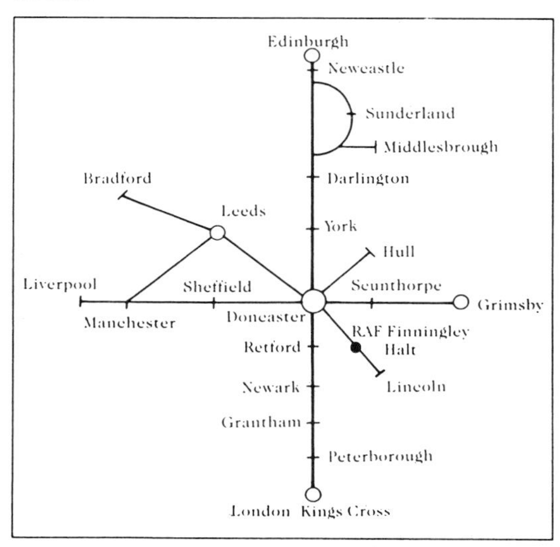

west of the station, itself requiring two river crossings. In fact, two other Roman roads met here, these being the Via Devana and a nameless one from Braughing (Herts.). The station here was the original terminus and was opened as such on 17th. August 1847 by the EAR as 'Huntingdon' until renamed 'Godmanchester' on 1st. July 1882. The village of that name lay about one mile to the south. Over the bridge was Godmanchester East signal box with sidings for Messrs. Brown & Goodman and Chas. Vessey, Fenstanton level crossing and both road and railway elevated on low viaducts, due to the nature of the terrain.

St. Ives station (4¾ miles) also opened on 17th. August 1847 was approached from the west and was situated where the line trailed in to the GER Cambridge line at a Y junction, with the signal box situated in the fork. There were platforms on both lines for the two directions of running and a footbridge for the Cambridge-Ely lines, which had a goods yard on the west north of the station with depot and cattle pens and, over the road bridge coal drops controlled by St. Ives signal box and St. Ives Yard signal box, the former removed by 1920. Firms having siding space here were Messrs. Coote & Son, Enderby and Fowler & Son. The town was close to its station which lay just to the south east. On the river bridge in the town was a chantry chapel.

North now on a different tack to Needingworth Jc., and the GNR & GER Joint line may be said to have begun again, with the line to Ely left running away on the eastern side, the Joint line next reaching Somersham (5½ miles) where there was a small station north of the road bridge and at the east end of the straggling village. Goods facilities were minimal here. North of the site was Somersham Jc., where the branch for Ramsey diverged to the north west. The signal box was again set in the fork at this point. The Ramsey branch came into action from 16th. September 1889, and was taken over by the Joint Committee on 1st. January 1897. The line was single with a passing place at Warboys.

About three miles north of Somersham was the quaintly named Billups' Siding ('Billup's' to the GNR and 'Billups'' to the Ordnance Survey) with the eponymous wayside yard of two roads and signal box to the east of the line south of the level crossing. Proceeding in a more or less northerly direction the line of route entered fenland as it approached Chatteris at 5¼ miles from Somersham, a good place with light soils for carrots, first the station with quite an imposing building complete with porte cochère and balcony on the east side, then the extended goods yard with depot on the east side and signal box with cattle pens on the opposite side. Chatteris village was close to hand on the east side of all this quite impressive installation. More was yet to come, however, some two miles or so to the north with a small goods station off the running lines but parallel to them, down to the Forty Foot Drain. A separate signal box controlled workings at this point. The loading facilities appear to have been fairly modest and for common use; a one ton crane was provided.

The next station was the small and neat one at Wimblington (3¾ miles), which had a rudimentary goods yard and shed on the west side south of the station and its signal box opposite. The solid, four square main building was on the west side. Rather surprisingly, the station was placed south of the village it served, when one would have expected it in a harder position next to either of two road crossings. The church here is a youngster of 1874, but of interesting construction in grey rubble, with stripes of buff stone. New cooperatives have been formed in the area to market a thriving potato industry.

At 4¼ miles March South was reached and the junction with the GER; thereafter was the town goods depot on the south side of the run-in to the station area, with signal boxes at Nene Jc. and Weighbridge before March East Jc. was reached, which controlled the level crossing at the east end of the station layout, as well as the spread of lines into the platforms. Basically the Up and Down lines went straight ahead towards Peterborough, with the side platform on the south side having the long, low main building. A bay was let into the west end of this platform. The Joint Up and Down lines curved out through the station preparatory to turning north towards Whitemoor, these having a side platform on their north side and having thus between them and the Peterborough lines an island platform into which two bays were let at the west end for Joint line traffic. In all, some seven faces were available for passenger use, while at the east end all through platforms were linked by a long footbridge. The north side of the station layout was completed by a turntable and standage for locomotives. The platforms were covered by typical GER canopies of the pleasing hill-and-dale type in glass and wrought iron. The Peterborough platforms were Nos. 5 and 6 and Bay 7, with Joint line platforms and Wisbech services Nos. 2 for Down trains and 1 for Up. The inset Down bays were Nos. 3 and 4.

March Station was a large signal box in the fork made by divergence of the two routes, while a curve beyond formed a triangle here and enabled workings to run between Peterborough and Whitemoor to take place, avoiding the station. Up freight trains from Whitemoor could use an Up loop which ran behind the station and came in at the level crossing at March East. The north apex of the triangle was at March North, and 300 yd. beyond was Whitemoor Jc. and the beginnings of Whitemoor Yards on either side.

Chapter 9

The Wisbech line continued away to the north east, leaving the Joint line to find its way through the complex. First up was the March Loco. depot, reached by a facing junction and curving off to a yard of its own at the west side. The original shed had six roads, with four out in the open on the north side and nine on the south. The origins of locomotive maintenance here are of interest. At first the GER seems to have kept engines at March on a casual basis, not particularly caring about the state of the small shed provided, while the GNR made do with a shed used by contractors, providing their own turntable. The opening of the March to Spalding line saw the beginnings of a proper GER depot which could hold six engines and had watering and coaling facilities, as well as stores. This was in 1870, and by 1910 things had expanded to the stage when capacity was provided for 100 locos., and by 1902 the shed could hold 24 engines with a total yard capacity of 107. The GER built two additional covered bays on to the shed described above, and concurrent with the growth at Whitemoor yards the LNER built a new through running shed of five roads complete with turntable and coaling tower. This new complex was set parallel with the down yard reception sidings and a short way north of the old shed but at right angles to it. The original shed was then used mainly for repairs. The nomenclature of the shed has varied between 'March' and 'Whitemoor' over the years, but both are one and the same, and it has remained important, with 186 locos. shedded there in 1935 and 148 in 1955.

Sidings at Whitemoor were originally provided by the GNR, known as 'March Joint' for exchange purposes. On establishment of the Joint Committee the yard was renamed 'Whitemoor' and continued under GER auspices until 1897, when it was transferred to GER ownership.

The flat crossing at Murrow, with K3 2-6-0 No. 61981 approaching on a northbound freight. *J. F. Aylard*

The system of yards at Whitemoor was vast, covering at its zenith 68 acres and with a stretch of 100 parallel lines across the map at one point. There were up and down yards, with Norwood yard, a traditional 'flat' yard, tucked in on the down side to sort out the seasonal fruit and veg. traffic for movement north along the Joint line. This yard could be indentified by the long goods shed, which formed part of it. Signal boxes hereabouts were Whitemoor Goods Central and Whitemoor Norwood Jc., with Grassmoor Jc. marking the north end of the complex. Once clear of these vast appendages the line descended at 1 in 708 to Twenty Foot River signal box, where the goods lines on each side joined. Here the cabin was on the west side of the line, with siding, cattle pen and goods shed on the other, the first of similar installations put in to deal with produce brought in from surrounding farms. At Guyhirne (3¼ miles from March), the first of tall and square buildings in the GNR house style was met with, a type not unattractive though somewhat gaunt in appearance, and which popped up in places right up to Finnigley. Here the building was on the west side of the line, with the signal box on the opposite

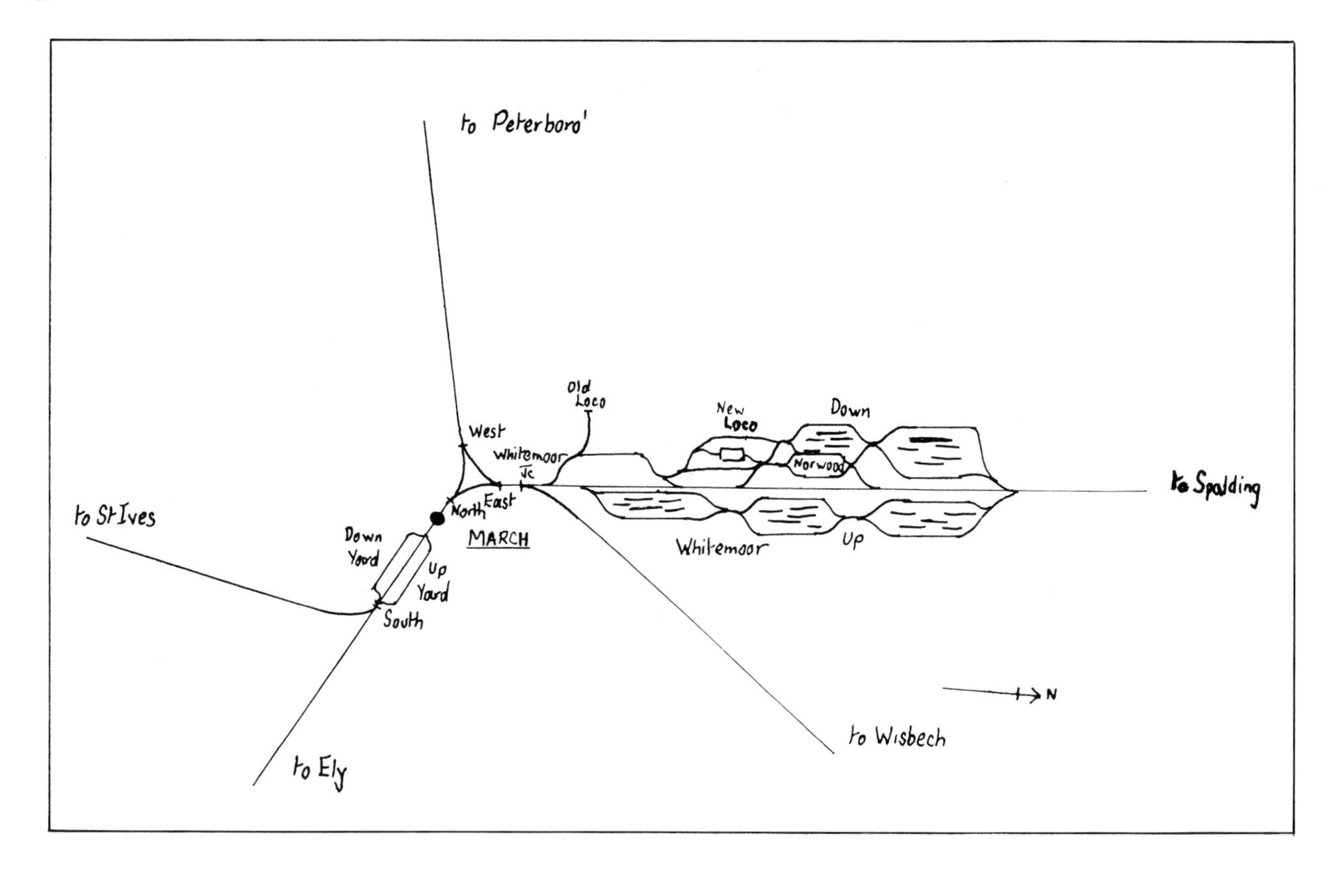
to Peterboro'
Old Loco
New Loco
Down
West
Whitemoor Jc
Norwood
to Spalding
to St Ives
North
East
Down Yard
MARCH
Whitemoor
Up
Up Yard
South
N
to Wisbech
to Ely

Class B16/1 No. 61424 of York passing Spalding with freight for March.
P. H. Wells

platform. There were no sidings or goods facilities at the station, which was in any case a long way from its straggling village away to the north east. Across the Nene river and after about half a mile Guyhirne Siding was seen on the west side, with two roads and a goods shed, probably built here as a more convenient point for customers. 'Guyhirne' was sometimes to be found without the final 'e'.

At Murrow (3 miles) the station building was on the west side of the line again with the signal box opposite and this time there was quite comprehensive goods yard at the south end of the station with a depot and a five ton crane. On the Up side was a long lay-by siding. The site was made more interesting by the flat crossing at this point with the single line of the Midland & Great Northern Joint line from Peterborough to Sutton Bridge, that company's station being further to the east and closer to the village, having a passing loop, goods facilities and cattle pens. Of the two, the GNR & GER station at Murrow was more inconvenient, except for Rogue's Alley farm just to the north of it, and, like Guyhirne, quickly closed. Latterly, colour light signals were put in between Twenty Foot River and Murrow West signal box, which was new structure built on the west side of the line just north of the rail crossing. The line now ran out in the wilds for a time as it crossed the fenland, making a stop at French Drove (2¾ miles) at a convergence of roads where nothing seemed to be in the vicinity to justify its existence except for the old sheepfold and a farmstead called 'Malice'. The station seems to have gained its name from the road leading to French farm, about three miles away. Unofficially the station had the suffix of 'Gedney Hill' for the large village 1½ miles away to the north east. This was made permanent as from 4th. July 1938. A little south of the station was a lay-by siding on the Down side, then came the parallel platforms with the station building on the north east side, the level crossing and goods yard and shed on the same side. With geographical fine tuning, the goods facilities fell on the Cambridgeshire side on the county border and the passengers in Lincolnshire.

Equally isoliated was Postland station (3½ miles) which, with Victorian optimism was originally named Crowland until1871 when it was perhaps realised that the town, at four miles distant, was a little too far away to be realistic. Whaplode Drove was nearby, but to use such a name would confuse with Whaplode on the nearby M & GN line to Kings Lynn. So, the station was named after the fenland district. The site was neat, with the station set north of its level crossing, the building on the east side and a lay-by siding on the Up side north of this. The ample goods yard covered both sides of the line to the south. Cowbit (pronounced 'Coe-bit' - 3¾ miles) was altogether more civilised, and was immediately east of its village and windmill on the Crowland road with, coming from the south, a Down lay-by siding, then the station building on the east side, followed by the level crossing and goods yard and shed on the east side. Cowbit was a collecting point for fruit and flower traffic. Latterly a loop was put in at Postland, and Up and Down loops at Cowbit for trains of up to 90 wagons. Cowbit Wash was, at one time, a great resort for skaters.

K1 Class 2-6-0 No. 62039 passes French Drove station on a freight.
Douglas Thompson

Chapter 10

After 3¼ miles the line entered Spalding. Spalding was, and still is, an important centre of farm production and market gardening and is an interesting, though somewhat untidy township as regards layout. For many years Spalding was the centre of potato traffic for many miles around, with

Spalding station. *C. T. Goode*

bulb cultivation commencing, surprisingly, relatively recently, about 1880. The railway was quick to seize on any potential traffic, with the result that flowers were carted by rail from the turn of the century, sent in the evening, either in small loads by passenger train, or on special workings to reach fast passenger or goods services at Peterborough.

This country had lagged way behind everyone else in the matter of sugar beet cultivation, which had been known to the Romans; then, after many years, the Germans extracted sugar crystals from beet in 1747, the first factory being built at Breslau in 1799. Napoleon encouraged the growth and processing of beet in France, so that up to 334 factories were working in that country for a period until his decline, when the industry also languished. However, the business was developed in North America until by 1890 some three quarters of the world's sugar had come from beet rather than cane. In 1909 the continent could field 6½ million tons and North America 400,000 tons, while the UK yielded not one single ounce.

In 1853 a small sugar beet factory opened in Ireland, closing two years later. In England, the first factory was opened at Lavenham around 1865, proving unsuccessful, probably due to the climate. Further experiments were made, and the first modern factory was opened at Cantley in Norfolk in 1912, followed by those at Kelham in 1920 and Colwick in 1924. In 1925 the Beet Sugar Subsidy Act was passed in Parliament, as a result of which the following factories were opened:

1925 Ely, Ipswich, Bury St. Edmunds, Kidderminster and Wissington.
1926 York, Spalding, Felstead and Peterborough.
1927 Bardney, Selby, Kings Lynn and Alscott.

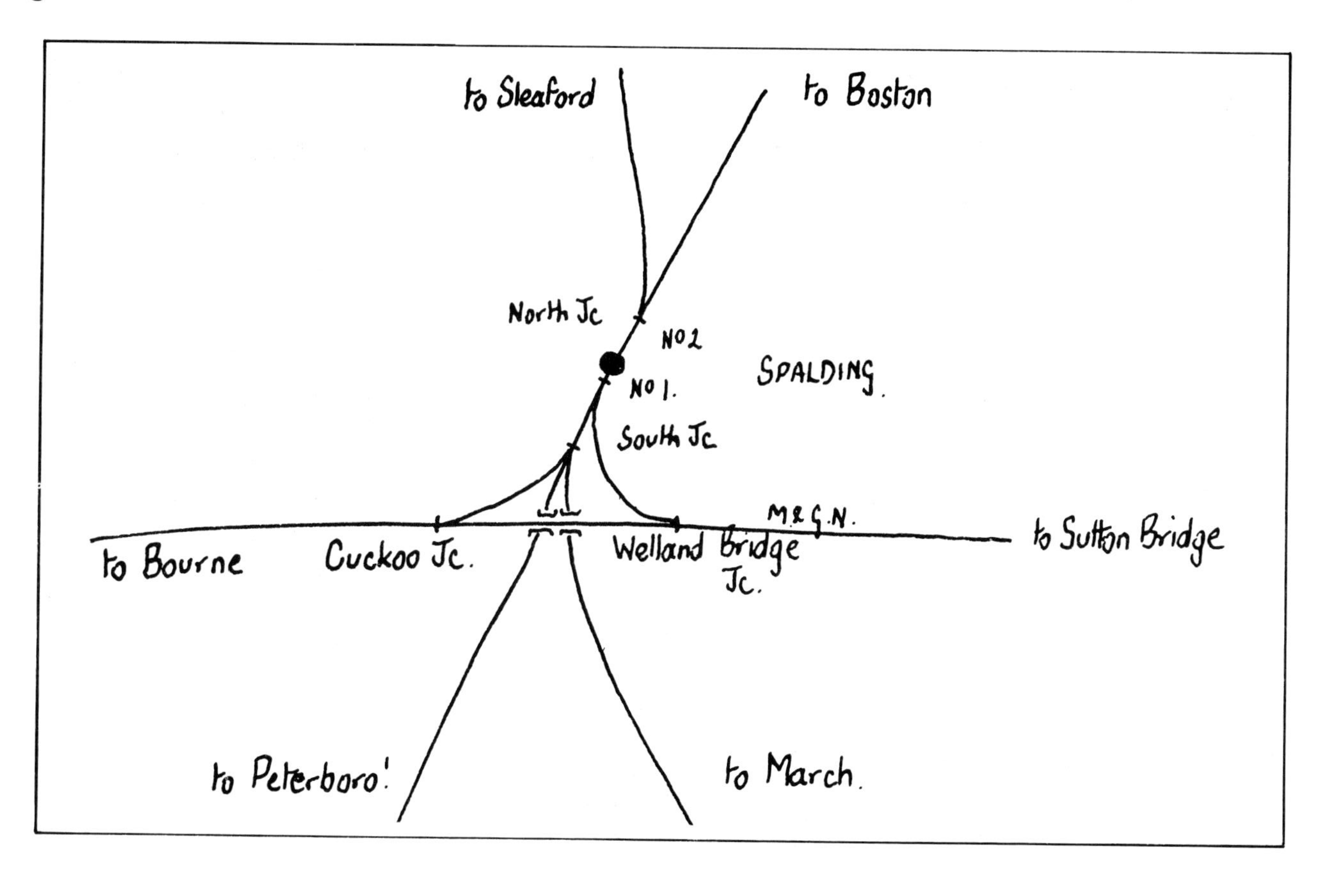
to Sleaford
to Boston
North Jc
No 2
No 1.
SPALDING.
South Jc
M & G.N.
to Bourne
Cuckoo Jc.
Welland Bridge Jc.
to Sutton Bridge
to Peterboro'.
to March.

The heaviest growing areas for beet, which covered nearly half the acreage of that for potatoes, were Norfolk, Lincs., Cambs. and Suffolk. Delivery of roots and soil, for which provision for removal is required, is carried out to factories within a span of 13-15 weeks between October and January, and often it was found convenient to store the roots in wagons at sidings up and down the line; even running lines were used for storage in some cases, overnight, leaving a single track. To quote one statistic: in the season 1927-8 some 126,000 wagonloads were cleared. Of course there was much ancilliary traffic, including coal and lime supplied to the factories for processing, and molasses, beet pulp and soil out again. Unfortunately, the factory at Spalding is due to close this year.

Back now to our route, which crossed the river Welland, then passed Welland Bridge signal box to run beneath the Spalding Avoiding line of the M & GN branch from Bourne to Kings Lynn. A short way beyond saw the line trailing into the Peterborough line at Spalding No. 1 signal box on the west side of the line, a busy affair which also took in the spurs round from the M & GN line by which its trains could call at the station, reversing in the process. There were four lines across the roadway at this point, which fanned out into Spalding Town station, first and foremost on the main GNR Grimsby to Peterborough line. The station lay just at the west end of the town and, as befitted its importance, had a good range of facilities in its long and fairly impressive building. The approach from the front was by a long driveway with intruding sidings and bufferstops, the same road approach as for the cattle and goods traffic, one might venture to suggest. The station had five through platforms, with a main island into which a single line bay was let at the north end. At its widest the layout was 18 lines wide and required five signal boxes, Nos. 1-5 to operate it. An interesting feature on the north side was the long Steppingstone footbridge which saved pedestrians a long walk round. Spalding loco. depot was a small one on the south side of the station on the Down side. At No. 2 signal box the Doncaster line diverged from the route to Grimsby and passed Mill Green level crossing and its signal box, where was also an Up goods loop.

Chapter 11

From Spalding to Sleaford the run was a flat 19 miles, relieved chiefly by the station architecture which was uniformly attractive throughout. Each building consisted of neat brick, twin-gabled single storey structures to front and rear, linked by a cross single storey building to form a whole, 'tied' from the railway side, by an awning to form an entry and decorated on the platform side by a full awning of four hill and dale bays carried on ten slender wrought iron pillars. The waiting shed on the other platform had a deep flat awning to match, and the whole site had a pleasant and opulent appearance. Sadly, in latter days the main awnings were removed, leaving an ersatz affair rather like the approach from the road. However, the brick buildings remained attractive.

The first of these buildings was met with a Pinchbeck (2¼ miles) a long and straggling village, always large with 3,000 souls in 1851, once a Saxon township attached to Crowland abbey, which might explain the large church here. It sat on both sides of the line, linked by a bridge across it just north of the station. The main building was on the east side and the largish goods yard was also on this side, with the signal box on the opposite side adjacent to the Down lay-by siding.

Gosberton station (2¾ miles) was also similar in its location, except for a level crossing at its northern end instead of a bridge which was controlled from a separate cabin away from the main signal box. The Down lay-by here was extended into a goods loop latterly, with capacity for 109 wagons, no doubt very useful during the season. Unfortunately Gosberton village was quite a long walk away to the east, leaving the much nearer and adjacent village of Risegate on the other side.

A village on the main road north of Gosberton which never rated the status of a passenger station, but which was provided with a goods siding was Quadring (rhymes with 'plaything'), where there was a signal box attendant on the level crossing and a long siding and weighbridge accessible from the two adjacent roadways.

At the risk of being repetitive it must be said that the next station, Donington Road (3½ miles from Gosberton) was in layout a rerun of the other two, with the road overbridge back in position at the north west end of the site and from here a ribbon of housing back eastwards to the small market town of Donington, rather sophisticated and set at the junction where the Grantham to Boston road throws off the road to Spalding. Matthew Flinders was born here, the son of the local doctor in 1774 who went on to become the great explorer and navigator.

B17 No. 61626 at Spalding with a down Cross Country Express. *P. H. Wells*

Delightfully rural was the signal box at Blotoft Siding, isolated in fenland with its level crossing and siding on the Down side and across rather surprisingly from the south end only by a slip from the Up line. Helpringham (5½ miles from Donington Road) was like the rest of the stations on this section of line, with a north end road bridge, Down lay-by siding and modest goods yard, though closer to its village than most on its eastern side. Beyond Helpringham were Great and Little Hale and, not too far away, the large settlement of Heckington on the Boston line which had a station of its own. This might explain why Helpringham closed earlier than the others, on 4th. July 1955.

Gosberton station. *Douglas Thompson*

From Helpringham the Joint line ran steadily north west for five miles to reach Sleaford station, more correctly stated as by-passing the town to the east and turning north, casting off a spur line at Sleaford South Jc. down to East Jc. where it joined in with the Grantham to Boston line through the station, then out from West Jc. round to the north to North Jc. and on its way again. The Avoiding line was worked on the permissive block system for goods trains, being made absolute block (one train in section at a time) on summer Saturdays for periods when holiday passenger workings did not need to call at Sleaford station. A diversion into Sleaford and out again added some three miles to the journey. Joint line goods trains from Whitemoor seeking Midlands destinations would pass on to the GNR Grantham line at Sleaford, with the reverse being of course the case.

Chapter 12

Sleaford is a thriving and cheerful little market town built on four principal roads, or 'gates', with the river Slea running through the middle. The station is well used and lies to the south of the town on the London road. The actual site had three platforms, No. 1 being the one on the north side which had the main buildings, a long single storeyed affair flanking a two storeyed gabled centre. Adjacent was a fine goods shed and yard, with a siding meandering off into the town to find the saw mill. On the south side was an island with platforms Nos. 2 and 3, the latter used by trains slipping in over the crossing at Sleaford East Jc. from the single line Bourne branch. South of the station site were five storage lines and facilities for dealing with cattle, while at the west end was a small turntable, a small two road engine shed and siding to a brass foundry. Sleaford West Jc. managed the Gipsy road level crossing at this end, plus the returning Joint line loop and the single line out to Cranwell which fitted in very nicely and which could work traffic on and off in a normal manner. The wartime LNER Working Appendix gives the following instructions:

'Trains from the Cranwell branch, after discharging passengers at the Down platform, must be set back on the Down main line to the Aviation Sidings. Before starting to set back, the Inspector or Foreman must obtain permission to do so by telephone from the Signalman at the West box, and before giving such permission the Signalman must set the points and pull off the disc controlling the Down Main line to the sidings. When a train is shunted and is clear of the Down Main line, the 'Cancelling' signal must be given for it from the West to the East box. Empty trains for return working may be crossed from the Aviation sidings at the West box and set back to the Up Main Line platform or Bourne line platform after the 'Blocking Back' signal has been given.'

The signal box at Potterhanworth. *C. T. Goode*

From Sleaford North the line ran due north to Ruskington (4¾ miles) passing Evedon Siding, probably a ground frame opened in 1882 to serve Sleaford canal which closed a year earlier, and itself lapsing after 1947. Ruskington rang the changes on the earlier wayside stations, having the same sort of road bridge to the north as well as the same attractive station buildings, but this time on the west side to face the nearby village, also the goods shed with signal box adjacent and yard on the same side. On the Up side was a long refuge siding. Between here and Digby were two wayside sidings, one for each direction, that on the Up siding being Bloxholme Siding, while the other raises one of those little problems which crop up from time to time. The large scale O/S map shows this as Dorrington Brick Works, though records show it as the Dorrington Hide & Skin Co. Sidings-possibly a profitable sideline at one time by the entrepreneurial owner. Whatever it was, it had gone by 1960.

Digby station (2¾ miles) was almost a copy of that at Ruskington, with, however, the signal box on the east side and with the refuge siding carried back behind the Up platform. The road overbridge at the north end showed the way in which it had been contrived into the setting by its bends, humpback and the remains of the old road which led to the level crossing nearby. Digby village was adjacent.

At Scopwick & Timberland station (2 miles) the line curved slightly and the yard layout and goods shed were on the east side to the north of the platforms, which had the station buildings set on the Up side. At the south end was the level crossing and this poses another problem, as all the writer's records show the signal box as being at the far north end of the goods yard on the east side, while latterly the cabin was down at the south end, controlling the crossing until burnt down recently. This somewhat radical change in the installation here can only have taken place since the end of the last war, and possibly as late as the closure of the goods yard on 15th. June 1964, though the style of the current signal box was traditional for such replacement to be as recent as this. Both Scopwick and Timberland villages were at good distance from the station, the adjacent hamlet being Kirkby Green. Of the folk of Scopwick, the village clergyman wrote in the 1830s that the women of his parish consumed too much tobacco, and that their children were tardy at attending Sunday school. Running north westwards the line passed Martin Road level crossing with its low signal box on the east side, to run into Blankney & Metheringham station (2¼ miles) situated just on the eastern fringes of the latter village and north of the former. The traffic potential here would be greater than at many places traversed so far, due to the presence of a large RAF airfield a mile away to the east, now closed, though the station was revived as 'Metheringham' in spite of the signal cabin stating 'Blankney' in 1975. Beyond the level crossing at the south end the Down refuge siding has been extended into a loop. The original station building was on the west side, as was the yard and goods shed north of the platforms. To add a certain savour to the site, the Branston RDC sewage works was adjacent. The original signal box here was at the north end of the station at the east side and was probably moved at the same time as Scopwick (above). An Up refuge siding was provided at the north end. At Blankney Hall lived the Chaplin family, a power in the land and with the important 18th. century Charles (what other name?) whose descendant Henry was a friend of Prince Albert. Henry was the owner of the Derby winner 'Hermit'. Latterly, the Hall became the seat of the Earls of Londesborough. Blankney village is full of cottages finished in the orné style.

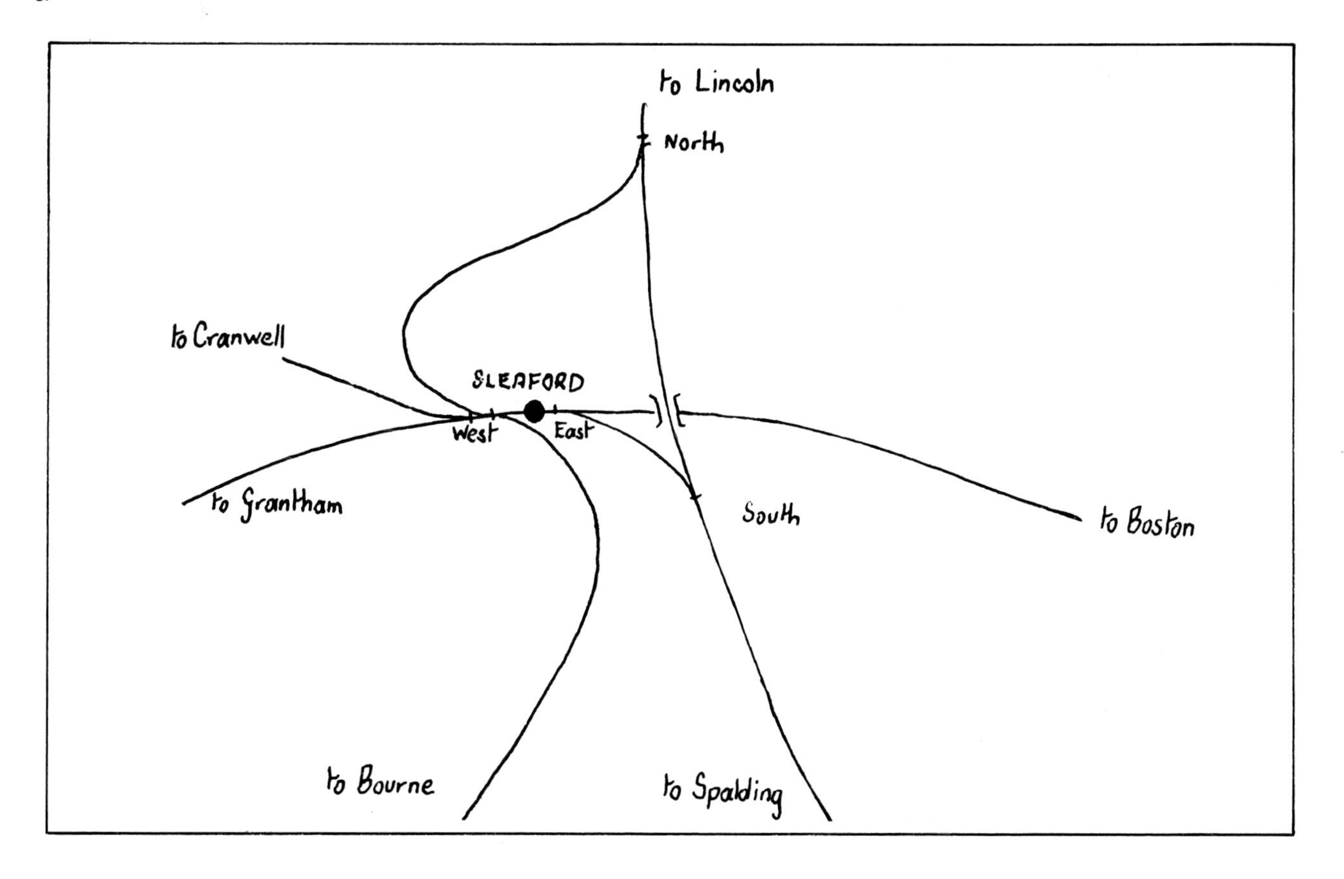
to Lincoln
North
to Cranwell
SLEAFORD
West
East
to Grantham
South
to Boston
to Bourne
to Spalding

Nocton & Dunston station was only a short way away, at 1¾ miles, and was spared both level crossing and refuge siding, most likely as the site was more restricted and undulating. The skew road overbridge and platforms were at the north end of the layout, with the station building on the south west side, as were the yard, signal box and goods shed. Dunston village was close by, while Nocton village, with its hall once the home of the Earl of Ripon, now a hospital, lay to the north. Mention should be made of the Nocton Estates Light Railway around these parts, a 2ft. gauge affair built in the 1920s to harvest potatoes under the aegis of a certain Mr. Smith, and extending up to 32 miles in track length. There are few problems for travellers negotiating the Dunston and Nocton Heaths nowadays, but in the 18th. century one was likely to lose one's way in foul weather, or even be robbed by footpads. Sir Francis Dashwood, of Hellfire Club repute, built a lighthouse, known as Dunston Pillar, ostensibly to guide such travellers at night, set beside the present A15 highway and complete with farmhouse and room for Thursday sessions of tea, cards and high jinks. On road improvements the light was replaced by a statue of George III in 1810; this, in turn, was removed to avoid hazard to RAF Dunston nearby in 1939. The statue is now at Lincoln Castle, while the plinth is still in situ.

The main line climbed at 1 in 737 from Scopwick to Blankney, then sharpened for four miles at 1 in 200 to a summit beyond Nocton, with a final six miles downhill at 1 in 400, almost to Lincoln.

The heaths were a rabbit area, that is, the animals were cultivated as a crop as part of a rota system, being allowed to breed in warrens for a time, before the land was ploughed up. Some two thousand couples could yield £100 profit per annum.

Potterhanworth (4¼ miles) lay about half a mile to the east of the station, which was set just north of the roadway passing beneath the line and having its station building on the east side. Both goods yard and fine signal box were also on this side, while a Down refuge siding terminating behind the station platform was provided. The whole site, set in undulating countyside, was one of the prettier locations. The spelling of the name is interesting, with the GER splitting it into two as Potter Hanworth, but Bradshaw giving one word. The postal address also combined the two as one, possibly the more satisfactory form. A Roman pottery existed in the area, hence the origins of the name.

Similar in layout, but without the benefit of a siding was Branston & Heighington (2 miles), set, for a change, in a cutting with a high road overbridge at its northern end. Heighington village was nearby on the north side, while Washingborough and its station on the Bardney line were within hailing distance. Branston was some way off to the south, probably the reason why the station was originally called Heighington, for Branston until 1st. May 1884

Chapter 13

With a fine view of the cathedral ahead, the Joint line approached the outskirts of Lincoln (station 3¼ miles), heralded by Greetwell Jc. on the right hand side controlling the Washingborough spur off the GNR and also the point where the Avoiding line left the lines running through the town area and

A ex GE Class D16 No. 62564 at Lincoln shed. *C. T. Goode*

the station. Like all the best avoiding lines, this was carried on bridges and embankments and crossed first of all the GNR branch to Honington and Barkston, then the extension of the MR line from Nottingham to the GCR at Pelham Street, ending up at Pyewipe Jc. and back on the main route to Gainsborough and Doncaster. Before this happened, however, a spur off to the right at Boultham Jc. reversing round to West Holmes brought goods trains into the yards which stretched back to East Holmes and the station. There was a GNR loco. shed here, while at Pyewipe Jc. were sets of Up and Down sidings and the GER engine shed on the Up side, of four roads capable of housing eight T9 class or 16 M15 class engines, plus the usual facilities and a 55ft. turntable. At Pyewipe Jc. the old LD & ECR, later GCR line came in from Chesterfield via Tuxford. The way through the Central station, used by GN, GC, GE and LD & EC trains, was impeded by the road crossings at each end; that at the east end, Pelham Street complicating the junctions with the GNR line to Spalding via Boston and the GCR line from Grimsby which also made a flat crossing with the station line to meet the MR end-on. The GC engine shed was also to the north of this crossing, for good measure, having four roads and a 54ft. 6in. turntable. Signalling here on a busy summer Saturday with heavy road traffic must have been an experience. Additional difficulties were created by the siding outlets from the engineering premises of Messrs. Ruston & Hornsby and Clayton Dewandre nearby. The station had six through roads, including two centre ones often used for coach storage or for running round, and three through platforms. There were four bays let into the east end of the north side, on which the main building stood, a rather splendid affair with a tower in grey stone, looking rather baronial. The main platforms were Nos. 5 and 6, with 7 on the outer face of the island, and side platform No. 8. Nos. 1 to 4 were the aforementioned bays

The Appendix gives the following instructions for Pelham Street crossing:

'When it is necessary for a light engine, or an engine with one vehicle to cross from the Up main line to any of the Down lines via the Through line just west of Pelham Street crossing, the signalman, after ringing the electric bell to the Gateman 3 times and seeing that the gate is opened, will give a green handsignal to the Driver to pass the Home signal at danger for the purpose of drawing over the through line points.'

Chapter 14

Once the Lincoln area was left the line ran north west with the Fossdyke canal to its right along to Saxilby (6¼ miles) passing en route Rowland's Siding signal box serving a small basin for barges with a single line off left, then Kesteven Siding on the right, where the distance between canal and line had opened out sufficiently to make room for a chemical fertiliser factory. The wayside station of Skellingthorpe lasted here for three years, from 1865 to 1868. Somewhere between these two wayside boxes was Fossdyke cabin, whose duration and raison d'être are unrecorded.

At Saxilby the line crossed the canal and immediately ran over a roadway to enter the station which was situated on the edge of the large vilage, once a canal stopping place and now a prosperous appendage to Lincoln. The main building was a distinctive stone structure, unique in form, on the Up side, looking across to the goods shed and yard which like Spalding's formed part of the approach. A long Down refuge siding ran behind the platform and until

Saxilby station. C. T. Goode

Sykes Jc. signal box. *C. T. Goode*

1922 the signal box was situated close by, whereafter it was moved away to the level crossing at the south east of the layout. With the later provision of an Up loop to the north, this necessitated much lever pulling, spring points and a ground frame to control entry to the lay-by. Instructions for the use of this were as follows:

'Down Refuge Siding. - This siding is controlled by a ground frame locked from the signal box. When on duty the station staff will operate the ground levers, at other times the guard will be responsible for this duty. In all cases the guard must ride in the brake van while the train is setting back into the siding. Immediately the train is clear in the siding the fireman must put back the ground levers. After train has come to a stand in the siding, the guard must go to the ground frame and be prepared to work the ground levers when unlocked by the signalman for the train to leave the siding, rejoining his train after it has been drawn out clear on to the running line and he has closed the siding points. The signalman must allow time for the guard to carry out this duty before lowering the Down advance signal.'

At Sykes Jc., 1½ miles further on, the GCR cut-off line to Retford went away to the west, the signal box being on a low embankment, before falling at 1 in 400 to Stow Park. Certainly, in latter times Sykes Jc. was regarded as belonging to the GCR section and something of a 'foreigner' intruding on the GNR line at this point. A small signal box on the eastern side of the line between Sykes Jc. and Stow Park was Sturton, which appeared to serve no purpose other than to divide up the block section.

Stow Park station (4½ miles) lay just south of the level crossing with the Roman road running east-west towards Marton village, after which the station was named up to 1871 when it was changed to Stow Park, with 'for

Marton' added in an undertone to avoid confusion with other Martons elsewhere, not that it mattered much as the premises were a good mile from Marton, a couple from Stow with its historic landmark of a church, but set in the middle of the old Stow Park estate. Originally, Stow Park house was the residence of Bishop Huge of Avallon around 1200. He is renowned locally as having slaughtered 300 of the estate deer at one time for a feast for the poor. The site of the house is now marked by a farm.

The station building was a stone structure on the Down side, with the signal box and goods depot on the east side. A Down lay-by siding was provided at the south end. From here the line climbed at 1 in 200 to Lea station, and to the west was some rather fine undulating estate land with hunting near the Trent at Knaith and Gate Burton, for which a siding was provided on the Up side. Here lived the Andersons of Lea, the Daltons of Knaith and the Huttons of Gate Burton. Only the last two houses still stand.

Station names do not come any shorter than Lea (2¾ miles), which was the place unusual in having to suffer a drop when the line was lowered here in 1864 to ease the gradients. The station building and four cottages were up at the level of the roadway to the west of the overbridge, while the station platforms, complete with waiting sheds and their awnings were down in cutting and were approached by flights of steps. An approach led down to the goods yard on the Up side, while the signal box and refuge siding were opposite. The villages of Lea and Knaith were at least two miles distant to the west on the A156 road. The line fell at 1 in 400 to Gainsborough Lea Road station (2¼ miles), passing Sir Charles Anderson's Siding (down side) and Ballast Road Siding, crossing over the same A156 by a skew overbridge to enter the station, whose long, single-storey building lay on the Up side at road level, giving a good excuse to provide a fine covered wooden staircase to reach the staggered platforms which were also made of wood. The curvature of the line round from south east to south west must have made the location of goods facilities difficult here; however, a top yard was provided on the outside of the curve, with goods shed and cattle pens, while a long branch trailed down beneath the approaching GCR line from the Central station to reach the lower yard with its GN & GE goods depot on the Trent and the Ashcroft Oil Mills and the Steam Saw and Planing Mills. Originally, one signal box controlled things from the inside of the curve, then this became North box and a South box was provided on the Up platform for additional sidings at the south end. Finally, South was the signal box which remained to become Gainsborough Lea Road.

Chapter 15

The crossing of the Trent was achieved by passing two signal boxes, Trent East and West Jcs., later reduced to one rather severe structure of brick on the eastern shore. As soon as convenient the Joint line left the hospitality of the GCR and ran on to Beckingham (Notts.) (2¾ miles) a station with a goods yard on both sides of the line, the platforms, then signal box and level crossing and the later addition of running loops on each side at the north end. Beckingham heralded a return to the station buildings in the GNR house style of slightly hostile appearance with pale lavatorial brick, the item here on the Down side and facing the village which was a five minute walk away.

At Walkeringham (1¾ miles) first came the signal box and level crossing, then the platforms with building on the Down side, followed by the goods yard, after which the line ran into shallow cutting. Walkeringham village was also close by to the west on the A161 road.

Misterton (1¼ miles), where the line now ran due north, began life much as the two stations traversed beforehand and had its yard with goods shed on the Down side, then its platforms with building on the west side facing the village, a straggling affair whose customers had a long walk and a long approach drive to tackle before finding a train. It was beneath the skew road underbridge on the east side that development took place, and where was to be found the gasworks and Ernest Newall's engineering works, both of which were served by a lower yard and for which a range of township-looking terrace housing was provided at Albion Terrace and strung along the main road. From here, too, the Stockwith Siding ran down across the fenlike 'drowned lands' once covered by sea water, to the riverside due east over the road to serve the works of Messrs. Morris Bros & Little. The signal box was situated on the embankment at the south end Up side, while the line from the lower yard came up some way beyond this point. Shunting movements were carried out within the yard by a horse.

Instructions to Staff for the use of Misterton Low Level Siding were as follows:

'Not more than ten loaded wagons and a break (sic) van must be moved either into or out of this Siding at one time. When the wagons are being put into the Siding with the Engine behind them, a break van must be in front, but when wagons are being taken out of the Siding the break van must be in the rear. A Guard must always ride in the break van.'

Misterton station. *C. T. Goode*

Haxey, a big village, or even small town, with a tradition or two of its own, lay a good two miles north along the main road from Goole, a centre of the old strip cultivation and home of vicious stinging insects called 'the little men of Wroot.' At the point where the main line crossed the road and began its turn westwards there was a little enclave formed by the station building and the oasis of the Great Northern Hotel. (2 miles). As designed originally, the goods yard was on the north side, complete with shed and signal box nearby, while on the Down side were a couple of long storage sidings. As the level crossing at the east end of the platform ends was quite a distance from the signal box, a ground frame was provided to work it, released from the cabin's No. 1 lever and also capable of operating the three most important stop signals whenever the box was closed. The crossing keeper lived in a cottage opposite. Haxey became Haxey & Epworth from April 1884. On 3rd. November 1904 the Axholme Joint line opened down from Goole through Haxey Town station in the middle of the village to a single line terminus called Haxey Jc. north of the hotel, complete with two or three sidings and access to the main line by a reverse shunt, in fact the final layout had a long slip right across all lines taking in eleven sets of points, excellent fodder for the model railway buff. When the rather feeble Tickhill Light Railway arrived on the scene, it ran into four Branch Down Sidings parallel to the existing layout and could reverse into three Up sidings on the same side of the line-or back shunt on to the main lines. Being at Haxey and finding oneself surrounded by all the equipment and railway lines (a stretch of fifteen across the layout at the widest point), must have been euphoric, and certainly not stressful except for a slight twinge or two at sugar beet time. The branch to Bawtry was 'one engine in steam' while the Axholme Joint seemed to be devoid of signals at this end, apart from the odd NER specimen. There was a run-round facility at the platform which had a single storey brick building, nameboard and paraffin lamps.

The Park Drain Hotel. C. T. Goode

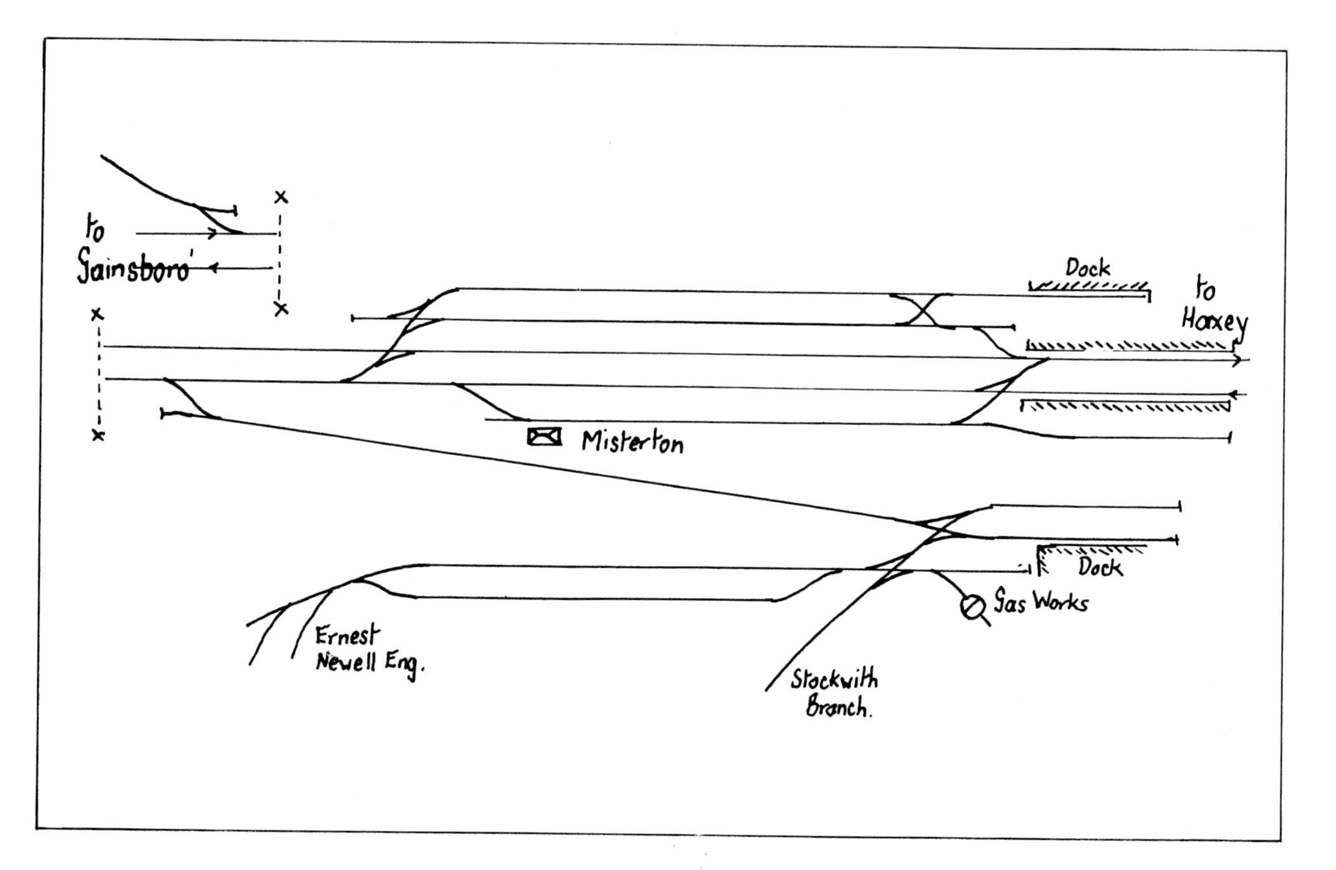
to Gainsboro'
Dock
to Haxey
Misterton
Dock
Gas Works
Ernest Newell Eng.
Stockwith Branch.

After the intermediate signal box of Idle Bank, named after the river, the next station was Park Drain (3 miles) at a truly desolate and windswept location with only the hotel for company on the north side, a remarkably hearty local structure of red brick which would look quite elegant on the hotel stretch at Southport. The sidings here, two on the west side of the level crossing on the south side, were opened in 1867, but a station of light construction was opened on 2nd. March 1896, roughly at the same time as the hotel. Refuge sidings were also provided for each direction. The reason why a station was provided here at all, as well as licensed premises, is revealed on the menu of the Park Drain Hotel, a worthy spot offering a good range of high class meals, if one is to judge from dishes on offer. The back of the menu reads as follows:

'The Park Drain Hotel was built in 1895 and completed in 1898 by Whitworth's Brewery at a cost of £5,000. The reason for building in this remote location is that a coal mine was going to be sunk. Unfortunately it was found that the seams were unsuitable to work on. However, after being built the pub has continued to operate with an atmosphere and character of its own. Now being run as a Freehouse and Restaurant by Barbara, Anita, George and Nick Sutherton. Our aim is to please the customers as well as when the proud brewery first built it.'

The nearest large village, Westwoodside, was two or three miles away.

Onward for a further three miles to Finningley station, set in Yorkshire though the village is in Notts. However, it was well placed on the main road for both its village and for Blaxton adjacent to it. There were sidings on both sides, with the goods yard and station building on the Down side. As often happened in rural locations, the signal box was at the level crossing away from the pointwork, requiring quite hefty heaving for all levers except for the few items immediately adjacent. With the large and modern RAF base close by, the station gains many passengers once a year when the airfield is thrown open to the public on Battle of Britian Open Days. West of Finningley was the small Auckley signal cabin.

The Joint line reached the end of its independent run when it arrived at Black Carr Jc., where it made a normal connection with the GNR main line. Before this, however, it played host to the Dearne Valley line of the L & YR which arrived and left by impressive flying junctions over the same main line and the Joint line; there was also a Down goods line and a refuge siding. A halt was added east of the junction in 1911 at an occupation crossing for the private use of the local golf club.

For the record, the names of the signal boxes from Black Carr Jc. to Doncaster station (7 miles) are given, controlling what was once one of the busiest concentrations of yards in this country. The largest were Decoy No. 2 Up and Red Bank, each with 100 levers.

Childers Drain Down
Potteric Carr Up
Decoy No. 1 Down
Decoy No. 2 Up
Red Bank
Shakespeare
Carr Up Goods
Sand Bank Goods
Balby Jc.
Bridge Jc.
South Yorkshire Jc.
Doncaster South.

A small loco. depot was built on the Up side, south of the main GNR premises on Balby Carr. This eventually became a wagon repair works belonging to Messrs. Bell, if memory serves correctly.

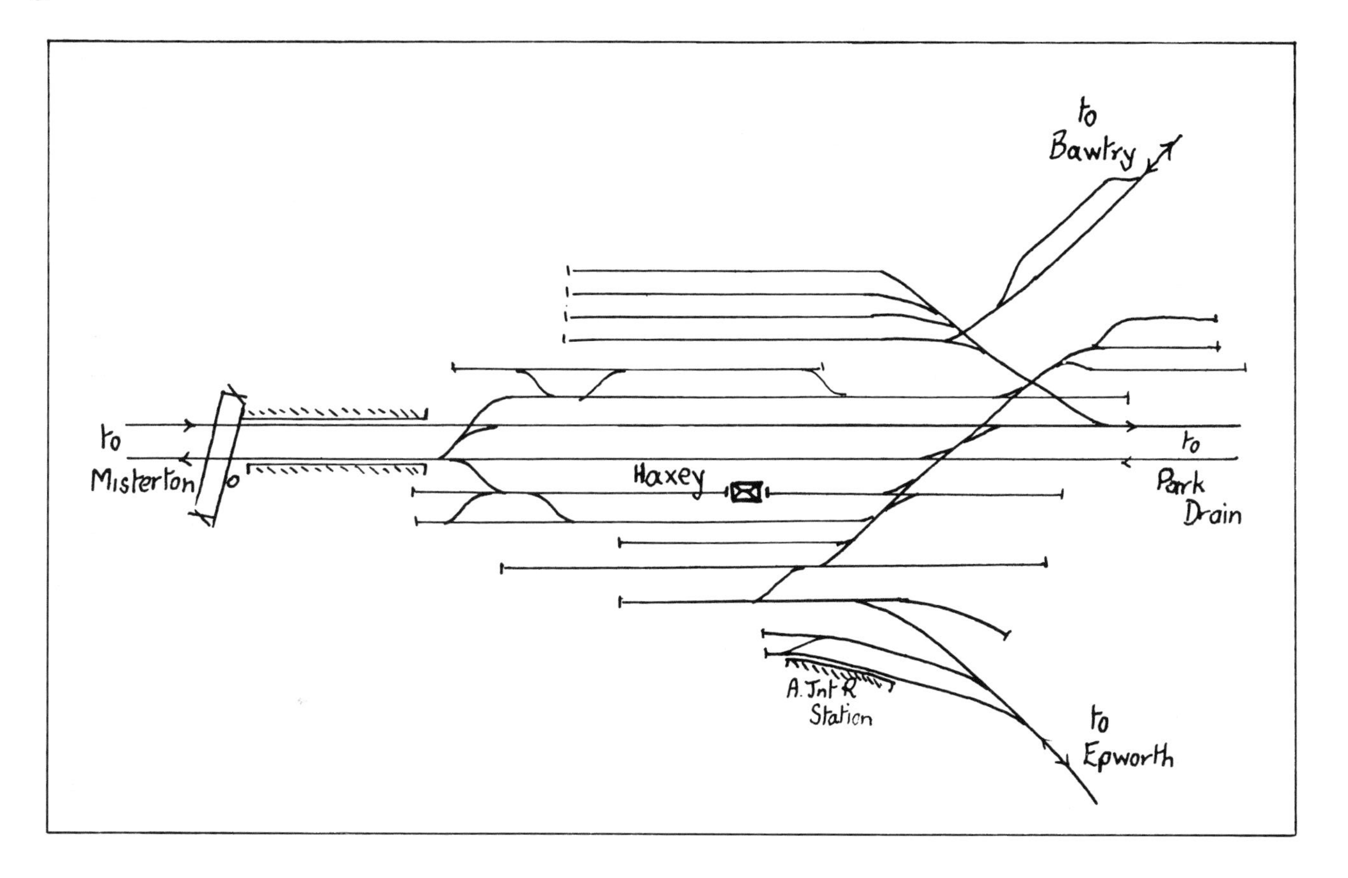
to Bawtry
to Misterton
Haxey
to Park Drain
A. Jnt R. Station
to Epworth

Chapter 16

The development of passenger services on the Joint line reflects essentially the spirit of things, with the GNR who were in the game chiefly because it existed, and wished to receive whatever financial returns were forthcoming, contributing little in the way of train services over the whole of the line. The GER, however, with a desire to expand services from East Anglia northwards into Yorkshire, went ahead with a will and provided what was to all intents and purposes a duplicate route to the GNR one, but which was nevertheless useful and practical. The more local sections, as for example that from Doncaster to Lincoln and forward to Boston or March to Spalding and St. Ives were used for passenger and goods interchange traffic, or as relief routes when required.

The GER set the ball rolling on the new through route by running a service three times daily between Liverpool St. and Doncaster via Cambridge, commencing on 1st. August 1882 and supplementing through coaches which had to be attached to March-Doncaster services. In 1892 the company gained running powers from the NER between Shaftholme Jc. and York, and three daily trains continued to run until July 1915, when they were reduced to one. From January 1917 the trains ran to Doncaster only, being withdrawn from May 1918. However, from October 1919 there was an Up working restored from Doncaster which was actually started back from York between October 1920 and April 1921. This too disappeared as a result of the coal strike. One persistent train which ran was the Sundays Only 2.35pm. Doncaster to Liverpool St. regularly between 1882 and September 1939, except for two periods between 1918-9 and 1921-6.

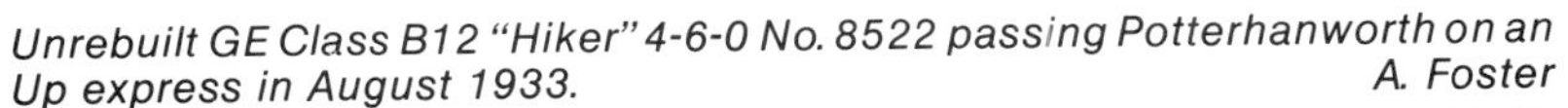

Unrebuilt GE Class B12 "Hiker" 4-6-0 No. 8522 passing Potterhanworth on an Up express in August 1933. *A. Foster*

Mr. B. Perrin gave interesting details of particular trains in an article written for 'Trains Illustrated' in 1957, some which are quoted here. Prior to 1914 the three down trains left March at 10.56am., 1pm. and 6.42pm., calling at principal stations, though the first ommitted Sleaford and the last called at Blankney. This latter also combined at March with the 3.10pm. Yarmouth (Vauxhall) to Doncaster. Up trains left Doncaster at 11.16am., 1.42pm., the first stopping at Sleaford Mons. Only and the last calling at Haxey and Saxilby. The overall running time to London by this train was 4 hours 33 min. with nine stops, whereas the GNR Doncaster-King's Cross line offered the 6.20pm. which took 3 hours 5 min. with one stop. Although no change of train was involved, trains between Liverpool St., Spalding and Lincoln were half an hour slower.

In 1914 the 8.50am. ex Cambridge reached York at 12.32pm., the 11.20am. ex Liverpool St. reached York at 4.25pm. and the 4.50pm. from Liverpool St. gained York at 10.09pm. Some services are summarised in tables as follows:

1895 *Down*

March:	7.18am.	9.53	1.25	3.02	7.27
Lincoln:	9.33	12.03pm.	a.	b.	c.
Doncaster:			4.23	6.23	10.37
Up					
Doncaster:	6.30am.		11.35		
Lincoln:	d.	9.45	d.	3.41	5.45
March:	9.45	11.58	3.15pm	6.13	8.04

a. Calls everywhere except Guyhirn, Murrow and French Drove.
b. Calls everywhere except Beckingham. Calls Walkeringham Tues Only.
c. Calls Cowbit on request, Saxilby Sats. Only. Express from Lincoln.
d. Calls all stations.

There was also a late run leaving Lincoln Sats. Only dep 10.45pm. for Sleaford, all stations, arrive 11.35pm.

1914 *Up*

March:	7.00am	9.58	1.26	3.10	8.15	12.16pm
Lincoln:		12.04pm	a.		b.	c.
Doncaster:	10.59		4.29		11.24	2.48
York:				7.35		

Down

Doncaster:	6.10am		11.33	2.10		4.00pm	2.35pm
						e.	f.
Lincoln:		9.47			5.48	5.13	
					d.		
March:	9.38	12.03pm	3.08	6.18	8.14		4.53

All above trains were stoppers. a: This was express, calling at Misterton and Haxey only, as well as the main stops. b: Ran express from Saxilby. c: Sundays Only. d: Waited half an hour at Sleaford. e: Sundays Only. f: Sundays Only semi-fast.

1951

March:	6.26am	11.33	3.30pm
		a.	
Doncaster:	10.10	1.51pm	5.59
Doncaster:	5.51am	12.38pm SO	4.50
March:	10.03	4.20	9.02

a. Arrival time in Lincoln, where train terminated SO.

1942			
	March:	6.30am	3.30pm
	Doncaster:	10.37	7.31
	Doncaster:	6.10am	4.23pm
	March:	10.37	8.24

The forerunner of the North Country boat train was also to be found, from Harwich, leaving March at 9.46am., stopping at Spalding, then Lincoln and Gainsborough, Doncaster at 11.58 and then York. In 1914 this train left Harwich at 7.15am. and was into York at 12.32pm., leaving York at 4pm. and getting back into Harwich at 9.17pm. There was a cautionary note in the timetable which stated that the service was likely to be suspended without warning, due to war conditions. At this time the 8.52am. ex Liverpool St. reached Doncaster at 1.16pm. and York at 2.09pm., with the 6.35am. out of York in the reverse direction getting back to Liverpool St. at 12.35pm. On Sundays there was one train each way between the two points, both calling at Haxey in each direction for some strange reason, unless to admire the extensive trackwork there.

By 1942, in the darkest days of a different war, the Liverpool St. to York expresses had vanished, though a Colchester-York train ran, leaving Colchester at 7.20am., reaching York at 1.30pm. and back from York at 3.10pm. with an arrival at the coast at 10.25pm. No doubt Colchester was the nearest discreet spot to which to run the service, and anyone military could quickly move closer to Harwich and its clandestine activities. On Sundays there was one train leaving March at 11.40am., arriving Doncaster at 2.30pm. with the return trip leaving at 12.30pm. both calling at principal stations, the latter adding also Finningley and Haxey, reaching March at 3.20pm.

By 1951 the timetable offerings would certainly have delighted the hearts of the progenitors of the Joint line, with a quite impressive range of summer Saturday services as well as the Boat train, which left Harwich at 8am. and ran to Liverpool Central, gaining there at 3.40pm. The return service left Liverpool at 1.15pm. and reached the coast at 10.44pm. The Colchester-York service persisted, out of Colchester at 7.20am. and into York at 1.33pm., returning at 3.25pm. from York and into Colchester at 10.25pm.

The range of Saturday specials reflects the buoyant mood of the time, when items such as a Cleethorpes-Hastings service were in vogue and attempts were being made to cater for and encourage new traffic.

To show the heady nature of what was on offer, below is a list of the return workings bringing holidaymakers back along the Joint line on a summer Saturday on 1950. Outward runs were of course similar: (All except * were Saturdays Only)

8.00am.	Clacton-Mansfield	arr. 1.53pm.
8.55am.	Ely-Newcastle	arr. 2.54pm.
8.55am.	Yarmouth-Leeds/Bradford	arr. 3.15pm.
9.50am.	Yarmouth-Leeds/Bradford	arr. 4.21pm.
9.58am.	Ely-Manchester Cen.	arr. 2.27pm.
10.45am.	Norwich-York	arr. 4.06pm.
9.45am.	Lowestoft-York* (to Newcastle Fri. Sat. Only arr. 6.31pm.)	
10.30am.	Yarmouth-Derby Friargate	arr. 4pm.

Ex GC "Fish" engine No. 5185 ambles into Potterhanworth with a vintage train. *Douglas Thompson*

10.45am.	Yarmouth-Manchester Cen.	arr. 5.46pm.
11.30am.	Yarmouth-Sheffield	arr. 5.08pm.
12.05pm.	Yarmouth/Lowestoft-Leeds/Bradford	arr. 6.45pm.

To add a little more detail to the summary earlier, the pattern of stopping trains on the Joint line indicates the quality of service needed and offered. In 1895 there were five Down trains leaving March at 7.18 and 9.53 for Lincoln, 1.25pm. for Doncaster not stopping at the first three stations, the 3.02pm. which missed out most of the stations after Lincoln to Doncaster, and the 7.27pm. which ran all-stations to Lincoln except Cowbit, then fast from there to Doncaster. Two of those delightful, though irritating footnotes (probably put in to keep staff on their toes) stated that the 3.02pm. could stop at Walkeringham on Tuesdays if necessary to set down passengers, while the 7.27pm. could stop at Saxilby on Saturdays to set down passengers. In the reverse direction there were all-stations trains from Doncaster to March at 6.30am. and 11.30, and from Lincoln to March at 9.45am., 3.41, 5.45 and a daring 10.45pm. to Sleaford on Saturdays only. No slow trains ran on Saturdays and time taken from Doncaster to March by this means was from three to three and a half hours. There were a few slows between Lincoln and Doncaster, one of which, the 9.42am. ex Lincoln, had the interesting footnote 'stops at Park Drain to take up wives of company's servants to Doncaster'.

In 1914 the 7.18 was now 7am. and the 9.53 now 9.58. The 1.25pm. ran a minute later at 1.26 while the 3.02 became the 3.10 and stopped everywhere to York. The last one, the 7.27pm. now left at 8.15pm. and ran express from Saxilby. In the Up direction the departures from Doncaster were now 6.10am. and 11.33 to Lincoln, plus a newcomer leaving at 2.10pm., probably the old 3.41 ex Lincoln starting back at Doncaster. From Lincoln the slows left at 9.47am. and 5.48pm., much as before, while the late Saturday service to Sleaford had disappeared. Sundays now saw one train from March to Doncaster, a semi-fast at 12.16pm. and a reverse working leaving for March at 2.55pm. There was also an oddity, a sole slow train from Doncaster to Lincoln leaving at 4pm. One wonders what somewhere like Beckingham could possibly do with one train going one way calling in the middle of a Sunday afternoon!

In 1942 there were two trains each way between March and Doncaster, the pattern remaining the same in 1951, with a midday extra on Saturday.

At the southern end of the line the GER introduced a new service from the Joint station at Huntingdon to St. Ives and Cambridge, while the Midland branch trains between Kettering and Cambridge continued, with a restriction on the conveyance of local passengers between intermediate stations. The 1895 timetable gives seven GER trains between Huntingdon and St. Ives, with the two earliest marked Mondays Only. From Kettering there were five Midland services to Cambridge, leaving Huntingdon at 9.47, 11.58am. (again Monday Only), 3.07and 8.17pm. There was a Tuesday Only service leaving Huntingdon at 5.07pm. for Godmanchester only, running empty to St. Ives and returning to Kettering as a goods train. As St. Ives market day was Monday, the reason for this operation would be interesting.

There were four services along the St. Ives-March line, and two on Sundays extended to Peterborough and Wisbech.

In 1914 there were now 11-12 trains run by the GER between Huntingdon and St. Ives with MR Kettering-Cambridge trains leaving Huntingdon at 9.22, 11.42am. on Monday and Tuesday only, 3.25 and 8.40pm. with arrivals in Huntingdon from Cambridge at 9.26, 11.50am., 3.32 (Mondays and Tuesdays only) and 5.16pm. On the March-St. Ives line there were 6-7 trains.

In 1925 Midland trains from Kettering to Cambridge called at Huntingdon at 9.36, 11.36am., 3.17 and 9.03pm. 1942 saw the restriction of GER services on the Huntingdon-St. Ives line to one train, out of Huntingdon at 7.45am. and one from St. Ives back at 8.55am., both most likely run to connect with a main line service to King's Cross or Liverpool St., while the March-St. Ives line had five trains. The MR Kettering-Cambridge trains were also down to two, leaving Huntingdon at 9.43am. and 3.11pm. for Cambridge, back through Huntingdon at 12.02 and 5.53pm.

In 1950 there was only one unbalanced train, from Huntingdon to St. Ives at 8.10am., while the March-St. Ives line retained eight, plus three on Sundays. The Midland Kettering-Cambridge service enjoyed something of an Indian summer, as below:

Kettering:	8.33am.	8.00am. SO	2.10pm.	5.20 SX	8.10pm SO
Huntingdon:	9.41	9.01	3.09	6.23	9.05
Huntingdon:	8.10am.	12.07pm.	3.13 SO	5.37pm.	
Kettering:	9.14	1.01	4.18	6.36	

Until its end, the Somersham-Ramsey branch fielded a good service of eight trains each way.

Chapter 17

The GER had provided itself with a brand new freight corridor between stations south and east of March and north of Doncaster, South Yorkshire and the West Riding and Midlands through the junctions at Sleaford. For all this the key marshalling yards were at Whitemoor, Doncaster Decoy and Mineral and Colwick near Nottingham. Whitemoor was, to use that overworked phrase, the jewel in the crown of GER goods handling, receiving freight for London via Ely or St. Ives, Ipswich, Norwich and Parkeston. Originally there were five flat yards at Whitemoor which needed local trip workings to place wagons and vans into their correct positions for forwarding. With the vast number of private owner wagons in existence prior to their adoption under the BR umbrella, the Down yard had the exclusive task of sorting these for return to the parent collieries. Latterly the yard became a holding point for express freight trains, while the Norwood yard nearby was used for coal empties, parcels and seasonal fruit traffic.

Ex GE tank No. 8553 shunts while a GN freight passes Pyewipe Jc. on 19/4/47. *H. C. Casserley*

The GER was quick to develop a good line in fast goods services along a route on which it was easier to accommodate freight workings since passenger trains were not so numerous, though in the beginning everything ran more slowly and much of it was loose coupled. In 1895 two express goods trains left London in the early hours, reaching Doncaster at 5.35am. with West Riding traffic and Down Decoy yard at 5.45am. with L & Y and NER traffic. In the late evening express goods trains arrived at March at 8.20pm. and 10pm. giving eventual arrivals at Doncaster Decoy and Mineral yards with traffic for West Riding and North Eastern destinations. The loading of the first was not to exceed 20 wagonloads, which indicates the importance placed on speed. Early on Sunday mornings two express goods trains left from March at 12.30am. and Whitemoor at 2am., both reaching Decoy at 5.15am. and 6.15.; the first had up to 35 wagons of West Riding traffic, while the second conveyed fish traffic for Nottingham, transhipped at Sleaford, L & Y and NER destinations.

Each weekday the pickup goods left Whitemoor at 6.40am. for Lincoln Pyewipe Jc. shuffling wagons at all wayside stations and getting there at 3.20pm., while at 5pm. a train left Whitemoor to collect all perishable traffic from Guyhirne to Donington Road, arriving at Doncaster Mineral at 9.50pm. Not to be outdone, as it were, the Midland put on an express goods between Kettering and Cambridge on Mondays only, through Huntingdon at 2.32am.

In the opposite direction things were similar, and among the more interesting movements was the 3am. Decoy-Whitemoor, arrive 6.35am. whose instructions were to clear goods traffic at Pyewipe, the 6.30am. Pyewipe-Whitemoor, arrive 9.30am. with the task of collecting cattle at all stations where required for St. Ives and the return pickup goods, out of Pyewipe at 8am. and due to stagger wearily into Whitemoor at 5.20pm. The author has a warm spot for the express beer train which left Sleaford at 9.35pm., called at Spalding and reached March at 10.55pm. after hours. One final train of interest was the Bradford-London goods which shunted at Whitemoor from 2.25 to 3.10am., terminating there on Saturdays.

Latterly, as earlier, express freight trains tended to run late at night and in the small hours, grouped closely one after the other for operating convenience. In the fifties the 8.40pm. Whitemoor-Niddrie was followed by the 8.50pm. Whitemoor-Ducie St., with 9pm. Class D to Ardsley, which did a detour via Boston, close on their heels. A little later the 1.45am. to Niddrie was followed by the 2.05am. to Niddrie (9.07pm. ex Dagenham Dock); then came the 2.15am. parcels from Norwood yard to Doncaster, the 2.20am. to Ardsley and 2.35am. to Mottram. the last two of which were Class D.

There was some bunching on the Up services, as below, where the arrivals at Whitemoor are given:

12.57am.	Class C from Ardwick	arr. 7.15pm.
1.15am.	Class C from Dringhouses	arr. 9pm.
1.55am.	Class D from Hull	arr. 8.40pm.
2.10am.	Class D from Ardsley	arr. 9.30pm.

The author has taken the times from Mr. Perrin's aforementioned article in 'Trains Illustrated'. If the trains were worked beyond Lincoln by the same crew, then there was a stop at Gainsborough for water. If te crew were changed at Lincoln, then water was taken at Pyewipe Jc. on the Avoiding line.

Chapter 18

To embark on a detailed recital of locomotive happenings on the Joint line would only be of great interest to the engine expert and would most likely only serve to bore the average enthusiast and seeker after reasons for the line itself and the impact it made upon the life of its own area. Sufficient, therefore, to give a few details which are readily available; the more recondite information must remain locked away. The chief motive power depots were Lincoln, at which there was a good variety of all types of large and smaller goods and mixed traffic engine to work in every direction, and

Near the End of its days C4 Atlantic No. 2901 in shed yard at Spalding.
P. H. Wells

March which, as mentioned, was a large shed with GER 'home grown' motive power, mostly goods engines. The slower, loose coupled workings north would run to Lincoln or Colwick and return in one shift, while the faster workings would reach Doncaster. Using the points mentioned as places to hand on wagonloads or to exchange them, a sensible system of operation was thus set up. Then there were the short, fast GER freight services to the north and Midlands, and the dawn of the era of the North Country Boat train which flourished in LNER days and afterwards.

After Grouping in 1923 the LNER began to displace some of its motive power from its usual haunts, and one railway in particular, the GCR, was to suffer upheavals as its more powerful locomotives superseded earlier types which, in turn, found their way into pastures new, displacing in turn older and more feeble machines. The GC 4-4-0 of Class D9 (LNER), a smart and curvaceous engine, made its first appearance at Lincoln among the ex GER D13s and D16s to take on the Harwich-Liverpool boat train to Sheffield, leaving there at 11.30am., returning from there at 4.18pm., having done a quick return trip to Staveley in the meantime. From 1927 ex GER B12 4-6-0s of Ipswich shed worked the boat train through to Manchester, while Gorton shed worked back with a GC engine, as far as March. Soon, however, Gorton was given an outstationed B12 as well (No. 8538 in March 1928) for a few months to haul the train. The Lincoln D9 was then given the task of working the York portion of the boat train until the mid thirties. In May 1935 the first D9, No. 6024 came to March shed from New Holland, an isolated case until 1939 when subsequent to the closure of Peterborough East shed, a further four engines were sent there. The last March D9, No. 6031 was withdrawn in July 1946.

The B12s were reasonably in evidence locally, with seventy built before Grouping, and a further ten afterwards, and even when Gresley's new Class B17 4-6-0s began to appear, they could still be found from time to time on the boat train, as No. 8568 was as late as August 1932. At first Ipswich had two B17s which alternated with one engine at Gorton on the duty, which entailed 215 miles each way. A Parkeston B17 worked between Harwich and Ipswich and there was a GCR locomotive for the stretch between Manchester and Liverpool. For both Ipswich and Gorton crews the job was a lodging turn on Mondays, Wednesdays and Fridays, and as far as the engines were concerned the Ipswich one had a far rougher time than the Gorton machine which retired to Ipswich shed on arrival. On reaching Guide Bridge the Ipswich crew was relieved and the train was worked to Manchester Central, where the engine was detached, serviced at Trafford Park shed and used on a local out to Guide Bridge before running to Gorton shed. For a time in 1938 the engine was sent out on the 7.22pm. Manchester Central-Leicester, returning on the 10.05pm. from Marylebone which left Leicester at 12.25am. Single B17s at Gorton included Nos. 2809, 2916 and 2834 with Nos. 2806/7 and 2825/6 at Ipswich. Nos. 2845-7 appeared at March shed.

Allocations of B17s during three periods was as follows:

September 1935	Ipswich: 2806/7/20/5/45. March: 2821/46/7. Gorton: 2816/41/2/31/12/47.
December 1938	Ipswich: 2805/6/20/5/45. March: 2821/9/46. Gorton: 2834/60/2/4/9/71/2.
December 1947	Ipswich: 1600/1/2/4/18/34/45/9/68. March: 1630/ 5/6/46/8/56/60/1/72. Lincoln: 1647.

The latter numbers above are the renumbered versions, though the last two digits remained the same. Nos. 2845 and 2846 stayed long in the same place.

After 1945 the train workings resumed something of the pre-war, with a Parkeston B17 running through to Lincoln where an Immingham K3 2-6-0 took over. From 1950 the Parkeston engine came off at March, replaced by a March engine running as far as Sheffield. The Lincoln B17 was employed on local runs. The last passenger runs made by the B17s were from March shed in April 1960, with No. 1668 the last engine scrapped in 1962.

Two of the large and handsome GCR 4-6-0 passenger engines of LNER Class B2 found themselves at Lincoln, with No. 5424 'City of Lincoln' there in 1936 and No. 5427 in 1939 for the duty of working the York portion of the Harwich boat train, which for a time ran via Knottingley in the Down direction and via Selby on the return trip. Until about 1942 these engines were regular performers on this service, then originating at Colchester. After Grouping some members of the ex GCR B4 Class, Nos. 6100/1/2/4 went to March for a few months to deal with goods trains north of that place, while in 1933 more of them, Nos. 6095/6103/4 were back again and this time worked passenger trains along with the GER 4-4-0s of LNER Class D16. However, with the advent of the B17 class they had gone to Lincoln by 1935, serving their turn on the York train working as above. Wartime saw these engines and others handling up to 16 coach trains on the Joint line as military traffic increased. Lincoln shed after 1945 was host to Nos. 1481/2/9 of the class. This was not the end of details of incursions by ex GCR engines, as in 1931 a group of small wheeled 'fish' engines of Class B5, Nos. 5181/2/3/5/7 and 6067/9/72 were billeted at Lincoln shed for sundry duties such as station pilot and taking trains along the Joint line.

Finally, mention must be made of the use, in 1923, of the service of various members of Class B8 which were imported to end a shortage of mixed traffic engines at March. Their activities were restricted to the Joint line. Nos. 5441/3/46 came first, then 5280/5440/2/4/5. All had gone by 1926 and their forte was braked goods workings, two of them to Pyewipe and one to Doncaster, the latter returning with a passenger train.

Latterly, the March allocation of engines included V2s, K1s, K3s, WD Class 2-8-0s and BR 2-10-0s (see appendix), and the workings included trips to Doncaster as well as a couple of lodging trips to York, an arrangement which NE crews working south to Whitemoor avoided by changing men at Doncaster or Lincoln.

Chapter 19

The Joint line appears to have been free of accidents during its existence, though two incidents have been recorded. The first was the derailment of GER 2-2-2 No. 295 on the 9.05am. express from Liverpool St. to Doncaster on 25th. October 1883. This happened at Kirkby Mount near Sleaford, and was probably due to the unsafe nature of the track in wet weather. Of the 24 passengers on board, half were injured. Light, fast trains were the order of the day, and after the opening of the line the GER put on six specials for the Doncaster St. Leger Race Meeting, including one from Liverpool St., raking in only a small number of passengers. The GNR, rising to the occasion by providing a competitive service from King's Cross, fared even worse.

The second, incident, vaguely amusing, happened on 9th. November 1883 when a gust of wind blew over the Potterhanworth signal box, leaving the signalman intact. Certainly the cabin would not have been today's sturdy and rather handsome structure, which still survives along with a goods shed adapted for other uses. Elsewhere there are cast notices here and there with GN & GE Joint thereon, to remind one of the past, as well as solid looking signal boxes at Finningley, Beckingham, Lea Road, Saxilby, Gosberton and Blankney. Haxey has virtually disappeared, though there are a couple of interesting coach bodies in a nearby field. Misterton is rather brooding, the station building surviving, as at several other places. Saxilby and Stow Park are probably the two most interesting structures in situ. Most of the station sites retain their main buildings, and Gosberton has its main building in good condition in use as a builder's office.

Of the larger centres, Lincoln Central has done well out of Modernisation, the building enjoying a £20,000 spruce-up and gaining the former St. Marks station traffic by means of a £1.7 million link line over a curve near Boultham Jc. The old Midland station had fallen into a rough state by the end, sheared up by baulks of timber and too near the bus station to be dignified. The main dmu. depot was concentrated on the site of the old GCR loco. near Pelham St. Jc. The station was left with five through platforms and the Down outer platform was dispensed with. The three bays at the London end were left in use for a time.

Peterborough – Lincoln – Sheffield/Doncaster

Mondays to Saturdays

		•		•	•					SX	SO						A	SX	SO		
Peterborough	d	0554	—	0657	—	—	0831	0933	—	1035	1033	—	—	1140	1217	—	—	1322	1322	—	—
Spalding	d	0621a	—	0724a	—	—	0905	1000a	—	1102a	1102a	—	—	1207a	1245	—	—	1349a	1352a	—	—
Sleaford	a	—	—	—	—	—	0930	—	—	—	—	—	—	—	1310	—	—	—	—	—	—
Sleaford	d	—	—	—	0742	0804	0931	—	—	—	—	1120	—	—	1310	—	1445	—	—	—	1606
Ruskington	d	—	—	—	0750	0812	0939	—	—	—	—	1128	—	—	1319	—	1453	—	—	—	1614
Metheringham	d	—	—	—	0800	0822	0949	—	—	—	—	1138	—	—	1329	—	1503	—	—	—	1624
Lincoln Central	a	—	—	—	0815	0838	1005	—	—	—	—	1153	—	—	1344	—	1519	—	—	—	1639
Lincoln Central	d	—	0702	—	0819	0849	1006	—	1053	—	—	1155	1241	—	1346	1355	1521	—	—	1612	1646
Saxilby	d	—	0711	—	0828	0858	1015	—	1102	—	—	1203	1250	—	1355	1404	1530	—	—	1621	1654
Gainsborough Lea Road	d	—	0723	—	0840	0910	1028	—	1114	—	—	1216	1302	—	1407	1416	1542	—	—	1633	1707
Retford	a	—	0740	—	—	0927	—	—	1131	—	—	—	1319	—	—	1433	—	—	—	1650	—
Sheffield	a	—	0829	—	—	1015	—	—	1220	—	—	—	1407	—	—	1520	—	—	—	1738	—
Doncaster	a	—	—	—	0911	—	1100	—	—	—	—	1245	—	—	1437	—	1612	—	—	—	1737

Mondays to Saturdays (cont.) / Sundays

			SO	•	SO	SX			SX	SO	SX	SO						Sundays			
Peterborough	d	1605	1605	—	1737	1748	—	—	1859	1859	—	—	—	—				—	—	—	—
Spalding	d	1632a	1637a	—	1817	1817	—	—	1927	1927	—	—	—	—				—	—	—	—
Sleaford	a	—	—	—	1842	1842	—	—	1952	1952	—	—	—	—				—	—	—	—
Sleaford	d	—	—	—	1843	1843	1805	—	1955	1955	—	—	2125	—				—	—	—	—
Ruskington	d	—	—	—	1851	1851	1813	—	2003	2003	—	—	2133	—				—	—	—	—
Metheringham	d	—	—	—	1902	1902	1823	—	2013	2013	—	—	2143	—				—	—	—	—
Lincoln Central	a	—	—	—	1917	1917	1839	—	2029	2029	—	—	2159	—				—	—	—	—
Lincoln Central	d	—	—	1740	—	—	1839	1931	2032	2038	2045	2052	2200	2222				1544	1730	1938	2110
Saxilby	d	—	—	1748	—	—	1848	1940	2041	2047	2053	2100	2209	2231				1553	1739	1947	2119
Gainsborough Lea Road	d	—	—	1800	—	—	1903	1952	2053	2059	2106	2113	2222	2243				1605	1751	1959	2131
Retford	a	—	—	1817	—	—	—	2009	2110	2116	—	—	—	2300				1623	1809	2017	2149
Sheffield	a	—	—	1900	—	—	—	2058	2206	2206	—	—	—	2348				1711	1856	2102	2234
Doncaster	a	—	—	—	—	—	1933	—	—	—	2135	2143	2252	—				—	—	—	—

NOTES

a – Arrival time.
d – Departure time.

A – Through train from Skegness.

SO – Saturdays only.
SX – Not Saturdays.

• – Does not run Bank Holiday 27 March and 1 May 1989.

Please note the colour shading columns is simply to help you read the timetable more easily.

At Murrow the links put in on the closure of the old M & GN across on 2nd. March 1959 lasted until 1964 for Wisbech traffic and to 1966 as far as Eye Green.

At March the passenger trains to Wisbech ceased to run from 9th. September 1968, and nowadays the station, still well maintained and beautifully painted, is now a stop on the Peterborough-Ely line with three through platforms and Down bays. The diesel depot is regarded as important, though not as active as in earlier days. Having lost its Joint line, Wisbech and St. Ives services, plus much of the huge Whitemoor traffic, March has suffered a great deal in recent years. The yards have been much run down of late.

Spalding has suffered much in the same way, with only the ghosts of the King's Cross-Grimsby service embodied in the dmu. trains to Peterborough running to either Doncaster or Retford in the reverse direction. No longer do the rather strange M & GN locomotives slip in and out with their cross-country services. At the time of writing, only the two through platforms on the each side are in use, while the big station buildings pursue a tenuous existence, liable to fall or be pulled down at any moment.

The Avoiding line at Sleaford is closed, and parts of the Grantham-Skegness route through the area has been singled. Again, much of the heart has been taken out of the operating aspect by the closure of lines which arrived at the station.

Sykes Jc. signal box still stands on the down side of the line and controls the now single line used for freight as far as Torksey, the future of which is in jeopardy.

Chapter 20

By the beginning of the 1980s it was obvious to British Rail that something could be done to make economies by closing a major part of the Joint line, namely that which was newly created as opposed that which had existed prior to the inception of the line. Therefore a proposal was made to discontinue rail passenger services from March East to Spalding South junctions, the direct line from Sleaford South to North Jc. and the Lincoln Avoiding line. After this document had been given an airing, a Public Hearing was held in Spalding on 31st. July 1981. In the first instance it was pointed out that no stations were to be closed on the main section of 19 miles 51 chains, nor were there any passenger movements on the Avoiding lines, apart from summer seasonal ones. Three regular passenger services would be affected by closure, namely two from Doncaster to Cambridge or Ely and a Sheffield-March service one way, and an Ely-Sheffield and two Cambridge-Doncaster trains in the other direction; however, during the season there were five trains each way between various points and Yarmouth which called at Gainsborough, Lincoln and Spalding. It was proposed to reroute these service from, or to, Peterborough and let them connect with a diverted Lincoln service, improving the status of Spalding station. One seasonal train, i.e. the Manchester-Yarmouth and return would be run via Gainsborough, Lincoln, Sleaford and Spalding to cater for the needs of holidaymakers seeking a direct service.

It was stated that nobody communed between Spalding and March. 71 objections were received, 46 of them from private individuals. There were two-declared regular users of the line, both ladies. Taking up the pleas of objectors: many of those objecting stressed the increased journey times which would be involved, and possible rise in fares for various distances. The ASLEF representative drew attention to the need to retain the line for emergency purpose and as a direct link between Lincolnshire and East Anglia. Difficulties would also be created by the need for passengers, particularly the elderly, to cross from platform to platform at Peterborough. The representative of the March Labour Party considered that money should be spent on upgrading the line and letting it complement the East Coast main line. Spokesman for the Railway Development Society considered that trains ran at inconvenient times for commuters, with hardly any advertising, and suggested stations should be reopened. As two railway divisions were involved, it seemed that the railway had been neglected.

A lady casualty officer at Lincoln County hospital travelled each Saturday from Downham Market (dep. 8.41) to Lincoln, getting back home at 9pm., a tiring journey but one would be worsened via Peterborough. She suggested that a maximum fare of £2 be offered one day a week, well advertised, and that by this means passengers would be persuaded to use the line.

Another personal objector spoke of additional congestion which would be caused at Peterborough by the diversion of 40 wagon freight trains off the March-Spalding line, while a Felixstowe resident mentioned the gradual disappearance of the Saturday-Saturday holiday precept demanding a good Monday to Friday service over the Doncaster-March line.

A pensioner said that, though the Spalding-Peterborough service needed improvement, it should not be at the expense of the Spalding-March line. She said that she looked for a reasonably fast service, on time and with the minimum number of changes or connections en route. Closure for her would mean longer journey times, worries about changing at Peterborough, whether the connection would be maintained and she feared that though fares would be increased. She would be likely to suffer the worst form of hardship, -'reduced mobility'.

Mr. Kirkham, an objector, thought that passengers from East Anglia were often incorrectly advised to travel from East Anglia to York via Peterborough when a suitable service existed via Spalding an Lincoln. He suggested that all services proposed should be through to avoid a change.

Various senior officials of BR then gave their answers to points raised at the meeting and these were of the customary bland variety, which for the most part justified closure of the line, seeming to regard closure as an advantage in some respects. It was admitted that journey times via Peterborough would be longer, except in the case of certain longer cross-country journeys. Of the lady travelling from Downham Market to Lincoln it was stated that, even with a change at Peterborough, the journey time would only be extended by eleven minutes. The waiting time at Peterborough in each direction would only be 8 minutes and 7 minutes, which would be too risky if the arriving train were late.

The official response to the likely problems of transfer facing some passengers with difficulties at Peterborough was that it was hoped that only cross platform transfer would be necessary, but should it be necessary for the disabled or elderly to have to cross to another platform, ramps were provided to an overbridge to the north of the station, for which a notice was provided, as was also a wheelchair if required.

In answer to a complaint that closure of the Avoiding line at Sleaford would lead to congestion through the station on summer Saturdays, it was pointed out that, apart from an odd service, all others could be diverted away via Peterborough. In answer to a logical objection that, equally, freight trains diverted away from the avoiding lines through Lincoln and Sleaford would cause congestion, it was pointed out, cunningly, that the hearing was being held to deal with passenger services; however, figures were given, for the record:

Freight trains passing over:

	Lincoln Avoiding Line	Sleaford Avoiding Line
6.00 to 14.00	6	7
14.00 to 22.00	7	7
22.00 to 6.00	3	17

The Department of Transport Closure Document is printed below (with acknowledgements):

19 August 1982

The Chief Secretary
British Railway Board
Rail House
Euston Square
London
NW1 2DZ

Sir

PROPOSED WITHDRAWAL OF RAIL PASSENGER SERVICES BETWEEN MARCH EAST JUNCTION - SPALDING SOUTH JUNCTION: SLEAFORD SOUTH JUNCTION - PYEWIPE JUNCION (LINCOLN AVOIDING LINE)

I am directed by the Secretary of State for Transport to refer to the proposal published by the British Railways Board in accordance with Section 56 of the Transport Act 1962 to withdraw rail passenger services between March East Junction and Spalding South Junction; between Sleaford South Juction and Sleaford North Junction and between Greetwell West Junction and Pyewipe Junction.

2. This proposal arises from the Board's identification of scope for substantial savings in track renewal costs by closing the direct line between March and Spalding and the avoiding lines at Lincoln and Sleaford. The regular daily services over these lines would be re-routed via Peterborough, with all but one of the present through trains starting or terminating there; and all but two of the Summer Saturday trains using these lines would be re-routed via the East Coast Main Line.

3. Objections to this proposal were received by the Transport Users' Consultative Committees for the East Midlands and for East Anglia. In accordance with Section 56(9) of the 1962 Act, the Committees decided that the Committee for the East Midlands should consider these objections.

4. This Committee concluded that withdrawal of direct rail services between March and Spalding would cause hardship to passengers who would face longer and less convenient journeys. There would be special problems for elderly and disabled passengers through having to change trains at Peterborough. The Committee were also concerned about the reduction in Summer Saturday trains between Great Yarmouth and Gainsborough Lea Road, Lincoln, Sleaford, Spalding and March. They thought that hardship could be alleviated to some extent by eliminating changes at Peterborough and running all trains as through services; and by running a second Summer Saturday train in each direction along the present route. In the event of closure of the line between March and Spalding, they wished the Board to give formal notice that all fares for journeys re-routed via Peterborough would be maintained at the equivalent level of fares on the direct route for a minimum of five years. The Committee concluded that closure of the two avoiding lines would not cause hardship.

5. In considering this closure proposal, the Secretary of State has noted that the Board would be able to achieve substantial savings in annual operating costs and also to avoid expenditure of around £4m on track renewal over the next decade. He has also noted that it would be possible to save some £400,000 of the cost of planned A. 47 diversion through Guyhirn if the line was no longer in use. These savings could be achieved without depriving any passengers of rail services.

6. In accordance with Section 54(1) of the Transport Act 1968, having had regard to all relevant factors (including social and economic considerations), the Secretary of State has concluded that refusal of consent to the closure of the line between March and Spalding, and the avoiding lines at Lincoln and Sleaford, could not be justified.

7. In reaching that conclusion, the Secretary of State has noted the suggestions in the report by the Transport Users' Consultative Committee for alleviating hardship to users. He agrees that journey times could be reduced and the inconvenience of changing trains avoided by continuing to run through trains via Peterborough. He has noted that the Board believe that it would be feasible to run a further three through services, and thus to avoid any substantial increase in journey times for all passengers and to avoid the need to change trains for perhaps a majority of passengers. He believes that any resulting increase in operating costs would be offset to some extent by revenue which might otherwise be lost, and he invites the Board to look very seriously at this option.

8. As regards the Committee's other suggestions, the Secretary of State notes that the Board have said that there would be no increase in fares as a result of extra mileage and he welcomes the Board's readiness to publicise that commitment. He does not think that a specific date would strengthen the value of that assurance. He sees no reason to challenge the Board's judgement that a single train in each direction on Summer Saturdays between March and Gainsborough Lea Road would be sufficient to meet the passenger demand. Finally, he notes the Board's readiness to offer assistance in the usual way to any elderly or disabled passenger who may find difficulty in changing trains at Peterborough.

9. The Secretary of State is anxious that, if possible, some alternative transport use should be found for these lines after they are closed by the Board. He is aware that procedures exist for consulting local authorities

about possible alternative uses, and he hopes that they will take advantage of this opportunity to look at ways of using these lines to improve local transport facilities. He expects the Board, under the terms of Department of the Environment Circular 116/74, to inform him before selling any part of the lines; he hopes they will also inform him before taking any action, for example by demolishing bridges, that might lessen the scope for conversion of the formations for some other transport use.

10. Accordingly, the Secretary of State, in exercise of his powers under Section 56 of the Transport Act 1962 and Section 54 of the Transport Act 1968, hereby gives consent to the closure of the lines between March East Junction and Spalding South Junction; between Sleaford South Junction and Sleaford North Junction (Direct); and between Greetwell West Junction and Pyewipe Juction (Lincoln avoiding line).

I am, Sir,
Your obedient Servant

J PALMER
An Under Secretary in the
Department of Transport

Appendix A

Code of Engine Whistles. (Extract)

Sleaford West Box:

To or from Local	3 short
To or from Western layby and Cattle Dock	3 crows
From Up Sidings	5 short
From Spur to Main Line to Grantham	2 long
Local and long Siding	3 short 1 crow
To or from Cranwell Branch	2 short pause 2 short
Up Sidings and Cranwell Branch	1 long 1 crow

Sleaford East Box:

To or from Boston	1 short
To or from Spalding	2 short
To or from Bourne	3 short
To or from Main and Local	5 short
To or from Local and Sidings	1 long
Goods to Spalding line	1 long 2 short
Goods to Bourne line	1 long 3 short

Pyewipe Jc. Box:

Single line to and from West Holmes	1 crow
Shunt line and Down Siding	1 long 1 crow
Shunt line and Down Main	1 long
Shunt line and Chesterfield	1 long 3 short
Up Sidings to Up Sleaford line	2 long
Down Main Sidings to Up Sleaford line	2 short
Loco. Yard and Goods	2 short 1 crow
Saxilby:	
Trains for Retford line, on passing	3 short
Sykes Jc. Box:	
Up freight trains having wagons to detach at Pyewipe Jc., on passing	1 crow
Haxey Station Box:	
Through trains, Doncaster-Immingham via Trent Jcs.	1 crow
Bawtry Branch line	2 short

Appendix B

Allocation of locomotives at March engine shed. Spring 1961.

D2010-2016	V2:	60803	K3(ctd):	61954	J17:	65521
D2030-1		60830		61963		65541/9
D2201-2		60858		61972		65554
D2237-40		60938	K1:	62016-7		65576/7
D3327-8		60948		62033-5		65583
D3491-2	B1:	61005		62037-40	WD:	90018
						/90208
D5043		61046/8		62051/4/5		90279/93
D5051-8		61052		62066-9		90305/40
D5062		61066	O4:	63687		90447/77
D5067/9		61095-6		63725		90484
D5094-5		61156/71		63746		90501/28
D5508/25		61203-5		63780/6		90559
D5531		61236		63803		90709
D5546-7	K3:	61810/27		63868/79	'Britannia':	70036-8
D5563-4		61831/5		63887/90		
D5568-73		61840/5	J20:			
D5578-9		61860/2		64690/1		
D5583-5		61886/90		64699		
D5620-1		61915/21	J39:	64772		
D5628-9		61929		64779		
D5655-69		61942		64901		
D8211-9		61946/8	J15:	65420/58		

Allocation of locomotives at Lincoln engine shed for the same period:

D2297-2300	B1:	61009/26	K3:	61807/28	J11:	64318/46
D2302-3		61042/58		61926/60		
D2404-8		61060				
		61202/58				

Abbreviations

GNR	Great Northern Railway	MSLR	Manchester, Sheffield & Lincolnshire Railway.
GER	Great Eastern Railway	LD & ECR	Lancashire, Derbyshire & East Coast Railway.
MR	Midland Railway	GCR	Great Central Railway
NER	North Eastern Railway.		

Other books of interest by the same author are:

'The Dearne Valley Railway'
'Railways of South Yorkshire' (to be reprinted soon)
'Railways of North Lincolnshire' (to be reprinted)